LEADERSHIP PARADIGM -
THE ETERNAL PERSPECTIVE

REFLECTIONS ON LEADERSHIP

Dr Prateep V Philip IPS (R) PhD

Chennai • Bangalore

CLEVER FOX PUBLISHING
Chennai, India

Published by CLEVER FOX PUBLISHING 2025
Copyright © Dr Prateep V Philip IPS (R) PhD 2025

All Rights Reserved.
ISBN: 978-93-67072-04-2

This book has been published with all reasonable efforts taken to make the material error-free after the consent of the author. No part of this book shall be used, reproduced in any manner whatsoever without written permission from the author, except in the case of brief quotations embodied in critical articles and reviews.

The Author of this book is solely responsible and liable for its content including but not limited to the views, representations, descriptions, statements, information, opinions and references ["Content"]. The Content of this book shall not constitute or be construed or deemed to reflect the opinion or expression of the Publisher or Editor. Neither the Publisher nor Editor endorse or approve the Content of this book or guarantee the reliability, accuracy or completeness of the Content published herein and do not make any representations or warranties of any kind, express or implied, including but not limited to the implied warranties of merchantability, fitness for a particular purpose. The Publisher and Editor shall not be liable whatsoever for any errors, omissions, whether such errors or omissions result from negligence, accident, or any other cause or claims for loss or damages of any kind, including without limitation, indirect or consequential loss or damage arising out of use, inability to use, or about the reliability, accuracy or sufficiency of the information contained in this book.

THIS BOOK IS DEDICATED TO

My family, friends, mentors and followers

FOREWORD

Leadership is about influence. In a world where integrity, accountability, and steadfastness sound old-fashioned, Dr Prateep Philip stands out like a 'city on a hill'. Unafraid and unabashed about his faith and his commitment to the God he serves, he exemplifies in his writing as well as in life a model of leadership that highlights the posture of a servant. As he has pointed out, to him 'good governance is God governance' and God governance adapts to the posture of a servant. This goes against the norm in a world where leadership is associated with power and popularity. In most models of leadership, we see and hear about the leader who becomes the focus and the centre of attention. What every leader will encounter in this book is the One who turned it upside down and redefined what true leadership is.

Leadership is service. To be a servant is the essence of leadership. That is the paradox highlighted in these devotionals. To be a servant is not about being powerless or without skill to fight one's battles, but the heart of the message here is that your enabling comes from God. To be a leader is also to be steadfast in this commitment to rely fully on God consistently despite the temptation to take things in one's own hands. The encouraging words you will find here will be like a soul-massage, bringing clarity and hope, building resilience and inner strength because it will lead you to the One who made you and formed you in His image.

Leadership is faithful stewardship. Every gift and skill we have is to be utilised efficiently. The responsibility we have in our hands as leaders and influencers is to be seen as our privilege to serve. Our call is not to lord it over others or use our position and power to exploit others for our own benefit. We are merely stewards of what has been given to us. In the large overarching mission of God restoring all things to Himself, we are but a small piece. What God looks for in us is our faithfulness and availability. The rest is in His hands. We are merely clay and soldiers in His hands. The influence or authority we may have been given is purely to execute our responsibilities. It is delegated authority and power.

Leadership is by example. The highlight of true faith is that there is a creator who exemplified what it means to lead. He calls us to do likewise. The call is to be the salt and bring godly flavour in the culture around us. The call is to be the light and shine God's holiness in our sphere of influence. A leader will not expect others to do what they themselves will not do. A true leader will not say, "Do as I say but do as I do!" The humble and courageous leader says, "Imitate me, as I imitate God." Leadership is about being an example without being afraid to be vulnerable. Good leadership is choosing to let people see who we are. It is about letting them see our weaknesses as they do see our strengths, because the One who makes us strong when we are weak is our empowering force!

Leadership is "others-empowering." If a leader is not building other leaders along their journey then their effectiveness is in question. Leadership is not meant for the benefit of oneself but for the benefit of building others. Leadership is meant to have a ripple effect of Divine influence.

To the godly leaders who place their trust in God, the road is never smooth and the solutions are never easy. Sticking to the Divine formula for leadership will push us to disrupt the status-quo when God commands us to. It is not about taking the easy road but about going against the flow. It is about being radical in a world of stereotypical norms that need disruption, so the truth stays, and falsehood is exposed.

Finally, leadership is temporary. In a world where people are solely focusing on success that is so temporal, godliness prepares one for eternity. Our roles as leaders and influencers may be temporary, but the heart of our faith is that we live and love and have our being in Him. To us our "doing" flows out of our "being". Our work here on earth is certainly temporary. Our roles, our position, our authority is all meant for participating in the work God is orchestrating to guide the world. Our roles and positions as leaders are ever evolving. There may not be permanence in any of our earthly roles, but our eternal call is to be worshippers. Being worshippers is our permanent call. If leadership is seen in that light, our burdens become lighter and our passion to serve becomes stronger.

As a social activist campaigning against colourism and gender inequalities, I have been personally blessed by the life and example of Dr Philip. I recommend these reflections of a faithful leader who has stood the test of time and continues to grab every opportunity to be a blessing through his God-given influence. I recommend his faith to those who may be inspired to follow in his footsteps as you read these life-giving reflections. May these words and meditations from his heart lead every reader to the God who made all the difference in his life and still continues to be the centre of his life. May you encounter the God he highlights and honours. May you find comfort, strength and perspective to be the best that you can be.

Dr Kavitha Emmanuel
– Founder of Women of Worth and Dark is Beautiful Movements

PREFACE

As partly intelligent beings since no human can claim to be absolutely intelligent, we need the help of our Manufacturer, our Maker to understand how we operate in reality and how we can do better with His help in all domains of life. My 28 book series lays bare our operating system and how we can access the Maker's absolute knowledge and ability to live better lives. The 28 book series is called The Alphabet of Life. It throws light on the Maker's perspective as never before.

The Alphabet of Life is the largest ever number of non-fiction books of a single author published together in a year. The reason I decided to call the series The Alphabet of Life is partly based on why Google under its current CEO Sundar Pitchai renamed the corporation as Alphabet implying Google covers A to Z of life. The Alphabet of Life will endeavour to do so. The series evolved out of more than a decade of prayer and meditation by me on a uni-verse or unique verse from the Bible every single day. Each uni-verse meditation attempts to bring out the meaning, significance, application and personal experience of that truth. Though the series will edify believers, it will help any seeker of spiritual as well as holistic truth come to grips with it and so be "set free".

"A leader is the one who knows the way, goes the way and shows the way."-John C Maxwell. The implication of the above quote holds good for God Himself, who does not require any pre-requisites in order to attain leadership, but He chooses whomever He wants. This is best exemplified through many known personalities who have encountered the call to lead and serve others, especially the ones who least likely possessed the necessary qualities expected of a leader. A leader is the one who is submissive in true service to the needs of one's subordinates, countrymen etc. rather than exercising one's authority and boosting one's power.

The book sums up the holistic qualities that build a leader and makes one grow in humble dedication and commitment to the work entrusted. It gives a profound example of the Good Shepherd leading his sheep and depicts the many selfless sacrifices required of a leader. It provides an understanding of how confidence and strength is derived through self-motivation and humble surrendering of one's capability and hard work into the Hands of God. Several reflections ponder over the fact that humility and faith are among the many virtues that enable one to fight strenuous battles and empowers one to selflessly rule for the well-being of the Shepherd's sheep.

A true example is embodied in the life of the God-sent Servant-King, hidden under a humble cloak, who took not a higher position to exercise power, but the greatest acts of service and love -this is what made Him a Holistic Leader. So are the leaders cast in His mould expected to heed to the call of every minute service. The book intends to bring to light the many spiritual gifts given to a true steward of God. In the view of growing as a holistic leader, the book provides a clear guidance on how God uses His power over His chosen ones to obtain victory through means of faith. The power of God is victorious in any adverse situation no matter how impossible the way to success may seem.

The 92 reflections provide a good read in strengthening one's will to fight for justice in the midst of adversity and lighting the lamp of God, thus proclaiming to the nations His will and vigour. For many are called and a few are chosen, those chosen are the ones who seemed less of a leader to the world but more of a soldier to God. A Good Shepherd contributes to the morale of his sheep. In view of this, the book focuses on growing more in simplicity of act and thought and being generous in provision to the needs of one's fellow men.

Dr Prateep V Philip, IPS (R)

ACKNOWLEDGEMENTS

*E*very good gift and every perfect gift is from above, coming down from the Father of lights with whom there is no variation or shadow due to change. A book is a fundamental leader that creates many leaders through the footprint it engraves. I am deeply satisfied to express my heartfelt gratitude to the many hands that worked together to bring this book to completion.

I would like to begin by acknowledging the generous blessings bestowed upon me by Almighty God in helping me persevere in writing each reflection over a span of 10 years. I thank my readers and the people who supported and encouraged me on this mission. I am indebted to her Ms Maria Swetha who laboured over 16 months, waded through 1.7 million words, 5600 pages of text to edit, proofread and classify theme-wise the entire series of 28 books, this being the fourth book related to Leadership. I am also indebted to for her support in this publication. A portrait captures the mind of the reader, so in this regard, I acknowledge the resourceful hands that went into designing this cover page by Miss Agalya and her Clever Fox team. A special thanks to Dr Kavitha, the founder of Women of Worth and Dark is Beautiful Movement, for the insightful foreword. I deeply express my gratitude to my family and friends for their timely

Acknowledgements

support and igniting the flame within me to take this forward.

We see the hidden leadership in nature as it embodies itself as God's artistic creation. Such a creation of God serves humanity. It perseveres in standing firm through the scourging heat and relishes the heavy rainfall to be washed anew. As the pages of the book turn, it essentially draws the strength of the Divine to be of good service to others than owning authoritative power wrapped in pride. I wish every reader to savour the role of a leader at every opportunity that one may encounter every day.

Dr Prateep V Philip, IPS (R)

CONTENTS

Foreword v
Preface ix
Acknowledgements xiii

1. Tending the Lost Sheep 1
2. The Power of Your God-Given Teeth 3
3. Obtaining the King's Favour 5
4. A Shepherd After God's Heart 7
5. On Lapping the Word 9
6. God Governance is Good Governance 10
7. The Transmission 12
8. Shining Stars In God's Kingdom 14
9. The Standards of the Lord 16
10. The Royal Priesthood 19
11. Leadership By Promise 22
12. Integrity of Heart 25
13. Spiritual Authority 27
14. Anointed to Serve 30
15. Three Functions, One Purpose 32
16. Feed Like A Shepherd, Graze Like the Sheep 34

Contents

17. A Good Soldier of Jesus 37
18. Using the Authority of the Author 39
19. Stewardship of Leader Gifts 41
20. The Dew of Leadership 43
21. The Test of Good and Godly Leadership 45
22. Being a Servant Leader, Not a Serpent Leader 48
23. The Sovereignty of God 50
24. The Little Green Light in Our Souls 52
25. Leadership Excellence 55
26. Weaned Leadership 57
27. Root, Shoot, Branches, Fruit of Leadership ... 59
28. Lion-Like Leadership 62
29. Active Leadership of the Lord 64
30. The Leadership Ladder 66
31. Our God Concept 68
32. The Jethro Paradigm of Leadership 71
33. Leadership - A Two-Way Process 74
34. The Legacy of Leadership 77
35. Triple Role- Witness- Leader- Commander ... 80
36. The Grace of Leadership 82
37. Leaders as Spiritual Watchmen for the Nations 85
38. Blind versus Visionary Leadership 88
39. The Priest-King Type of Leadership 92

Contents

40. God's Leadership and Godly Leadership 95
41. Leader as Watchman 98
42. Leadership from Strength to Strength 100
43. God Governance and Self Leadership 103
44. Supernatural Leadership 106
45. Fail Proof Rock Solid Leadership 109
46. Leaders are Climate Changers 112
47. Destined for Leadership 115
48. Leadership and the Power to Bless 118
49. Metamorphic Leadership 121
50. Be a Star Leader 124
51. Eagle-like Leadership.. 127
52. Headship and Leadership 130
53. The Inner Lamp of Leadership 132
54. Leadership is Headship not Tailship 134
55. The Leadership Tree... 138
56. The Holy Ground of Life and Leadership 141
57. Leadership Traits 144
58. The Light of Leadership 147
59. The Servant Leader versus the Serpent Leader..... 150
60. The Accountability and Source of Leadership 155
61. A Ruler after God's Heart 157
62. The Leadership Triangle....................................... 159

Contents

63. The Manger Leader's Source of Power 161
64. The Manger Leader's Source of Strength 163
65. Leadership by Grace 165
66. Five Dimensions of Balanced and Effective Leadership 167
67. The Image of the Human Leader 170
68. Lion-Like Leadership 172
69. The Ship called Leadership 174
70. Level Ground Leadership 176
71. True Leadership 178
72. The Pattern of Authority and Power 180
73. Patterns of Leadership 183
74. The Leadership Mantle 186
75. The Alpha of Dominion 188
76. The Alpha of Kingship 191
77. The Alpha of the True Leader 194
78. Stellar Leaders in Pole Positions 196
79. Absolute Power that does not Corrupt................ 198
80. Feeding the Flock 201
81. To Lead with Diligence, to Serve with Joy 203
82. Contrasting Models of Leadership 205
83. Be a Mentor, not a Tormentor 207
84. The Role of Godly Leaders and Prophets 209

Contents

85. Brand New Leadership 211
86. The Authority of the Author of Life 213
87. Ability with Stability 216
88. Intuitive Leadership and Wisdom 218
89. Wonderful Power, Authority and Government .. 220
90. The Authority of Jesus 224
91. Being Spirit Led 226
92. Authority over the Serpent Leader 228

1. TENDING THE LOST SHEEP

"BE THOU DILIGENT TO KNOW THE STATE OF THY FLOCKS AND LOOK WELL TO THY HERDS."

– **Proverbs 27:23**

Our leadership style must be that of a shepherd-king. David was a shepherd-king. Jesus is a Shepherd-King. We must be diligent in knowing not just the number of sheep in our flock but also the state of the flock and indeed, the state of each sheep or believer in the church. A shepherd is aware of the threats the flock is facing at any given moment and takes proactive steps to defend them from becoming prey. Similarly, we too must evaluate the threats the flock faces and take steps to thwart the threats. We must ensure the fencing around the pen is close enough and without gaps for the foxes of deceit and cunning and strife to enter. Our prayer must be proactive and protective. As the Lord Jesus Himself prayed, "Let none of the sheep be lost."

We must always feed the sheep. Peter was asked repeatedly to feed the Lord's sheep as a mark of his love. We feed the sheep with the Word of God. We must not look to our own profiting from the sheep but look to the well-being of the flock. We must be courageous like David to snatch the sheep from the jaws of an attacking lion (sin, sickness, death). We must multiply the Father's sheep like Jacob increased the flock of Laban, his father-in-law.

We must not while away our time as the sheep graze in different pastures (professions, careers) but keep harping on praising the Lord, as David did, for what He has done in the midst of the flock and the life of each believer.

2. THE POWER OF YOUR GOD-GIVEN TEETH

"BEHOLD, I WILL MAKE THEE A NEW SHARP THRESHING INSTRUMENT HAVING TEETH: THOU SHALT THRESH THE MOUNTAINS AND BEAT THEM SMALL AND SHALT MAKE THE HILLS AS CHAFF."

– **Isaiah 41:15**

The spiritual nation of Israel comprised of people of all nationalities and individual believers are like a new sharp threshing instrument that by incessant prayer, supplications, intercession and praise and worship will reduce all problems, challenges and difficulties (spiritual, physical, emotional, financial, relational) to size and dimension that they no longer seem insurmountable. The small and vexatious issues that used to nag us will also disappear. We need to ask ourselves, "Which are our big mountains?" and thresh them into smaller ones. We need to ask "what are our small problems?" and blow them away with the breath of God. The exercise of spiritual authority that is vested in every believer is like sharpening the teeth of the instrumentality of our faith. We must rejoice when we set our eyes upon our Goliaths as our level of success is determined by the size of our enemy.

The bigger the enemy, the opposing force that God allows in our lives, the bigger our ultimate triumph and testimony. Unlike the slaying of Goliath, our present-day Goliaths are not slain in one fell blow but by a process of steady erosion till they become like chaff that the wind blows away. The process of overcoming implies that we need to focus and stay with the problem, focused as an ironsmith would till the iron smelts in the furnace. We will feel the heat but we will not melt. We are not toothless as Almighty El Shaddai is with us and in us. He will sharpen our teeth against the onslaught of the mighty. He will deliver them into our hands. Finally, we just need to blow on the chaff and it will fly off like sawdust as if it never existed. The two sets of canines that the Lord gives us to bite are the Word of God and the Word of testimony (of how we applied God's Word in our lives). Yes indeed, we shall overcome by means of these sharpened teeth.

3. OBTAINING THE KING'S FAVOUR

"O LORD, I BESEECH THEE, LET NOW THINE EAR BE ATTENTIVE TO THE PRAYER OF THY SERVANT AND TO THE PRAYER OF THY SERVANTS, WHO DESIRE TO FEAR THY NAME AND PROSPER, I PRAY THEE, THY SERVANT THIS DAY AND GRANT HIM MERCY IN THE SIGHT OF THIS MAN. FOR I WAS THE KING'S CUPBEARER."

– **Nehemiah 1:11**

We are all called to be servant leaders. As servant leaders, we often need the "king's favour," implying the favour of persons in higher positions of influence or authority who can grant or facilitate what we desire for the Kingdom of God, for ourselves and the people of God. In the corporate context, it could mean the boss's favour. When we beseech the Lord to grant us grace to find such favour in the "king's eyes," He will cause it to happen even as Nehemiah found favour with King Xerxes in the Persian empire. He will prosper us in our way as He is Jehovah Shalom.

When we come to think of it, we are each a cupbearer to the king, in the sense that on account of our intimacy with God, we are in a position to influence the life, career and decisions of the king through our prayers. We can influence the policies of governments towards the poor, towards the children of God and other matters through focused prayer. We can influence the world and national events. We can influence the US President in the White House through the combined effect of our prayers. Nehemiah was not alone in praying. He had a backup of prayer warriors praying on the same lines. Their common quality was that they desired to fear the Lord. They were not motivated by selfish ambition but desired to be used by God, through God and for God. Interestingly, a good number of readers of the uni-verse have formed a prayer group called Hedge to pray for each other's needs and for others.

In my personal walk, I have found amazing answers to prayers over the past years in which the Lord turned the "king's eyes" to look with favour upon my requests. Once in the middle of a conference, when some adversaries were conspiring to disrupt an initiative that I had started, I cried out in my heart to the Lord, "You who can change a river's course, who can easily change a ruler's heart and mind, please let my plea find favour…" The one who is called Lord Amen caused it to so happen. After all, He is the Eternal King all mortal kings look to even as a cupbearer looks to the king.

4. A SHEPHERD AFTER GOD'S HEART

"I WILL GIVE YOU PASTORS ACCORDING TO MINE HEART, WHICH SHALL FEED YOU WITH KNOWLEDGE AND UNDERSTANDING."

– Jeremiah 3:15

The word "pastor" comes from "shepherd" or the one who takes the sheep to the pasture to feed. Jesus is the Chief Shepherd but in every generation, He has anointed shepherds over His flock who are imbued with knowledge and understanding and fed the flock from the Word of God. All of the pastors start off as sheep or as believers but are groomed by the Lord over a period of time to become transformed into shepherds. A shepherd must be moulded after God's own heart, loving, caring, considerate and humble. From the Lord's perspective, feeding the sheep or believers with the Word of God is the equivalent of leadership. A shepherd must be devoted to the well-being of the last person in his flock like the shepherd who went looking for the lost sheep. A shepherd who is a hireling is more interested in the profit or the lucre that the sheep will bring in.

Such a hireling is only interested in shearing the sheep of their earnings and not in defending or providing or feeding them. In contrast, a true shepherd or pastor is not interested in self-aggrandisement or self-glorification but in reflecting the love of the very heart of God. A shepherd needs two gifts: the word of knowledge and the word of wisdom. He must know the apt portion of scripture to share at the needed time. He must also be sensitive to the needs of others and be able to give wise counsel. Knowledge of the Word accompanied by a deep understanding of people will enable a shepherd or pastor to be effective. The Lord promises to give such faithful pastors who would lead or feed the sheep.

5. ON LAPPING THE WORD

"SO GIDEON TOOK THE MEN DOWN TO THE WATER. THERE THE LORD TOLD HIM, 'SEPARATE THOSE WHO LAP THE WATER WITH THEIR TONGUES LIKE A DOG FROM THOSE WHO KNEEL TO DRINK.'"

– Judges 7:5

Once the Lord said, "You are like a dog that laps my Word as if it is precious milk." The image can be understood when we visualise a dog drinking milk from a vessel and a dog drinking water. The dog that drinks the milk laps it up with a lot of joy and gusto till it laps up the last drop while the dog that drinks the water will move away after licking the surface of the water a few times. Even the dog knows that milk is precious, valuable and rare while water is copious and easily obtainable. The Lord helped Gideon to sift and sort the volunteer troops by how they drank the water. Similarly, we can today sift and sort teams by how they deal with the Word of God. Are they superficial and lukewarm in their attitude and intake of the Word or are they eager and enthusiastic? I often pray, "Lord please sift and sort the leaders and teachers of the church and in the world." Leaders should be firebrands like Gideon's troops. We should be torches of "Holy Spirit fire" within the earthen pots that are our bodies.

6. GOD GOVERNANCE IS GOOD GOVERNANCE

"FOR THE LORD IS OUR JUDGE, THE LORD IS OUR LAWGIVER, THE LORD IS OUR KING, HE WILL SAVE US."

– Isaiah 33:22

The three branches of governance traditionally are Legislature - the law-giver, the Executive-that executes laws and the Judiciary that adjudicates law. This uni-verse acknowledges God as the ultimate law-giver, executor and Judge. True and original sovereign power rests in and with God. As a King, He is just, humble, accessible and generous. As an ultimate ruler, He decides to remove one earthly ruler and bring up another. The Bible is the fundamental law or Constitution of the Kingdom of God. Unlike the Constitutions of the nations of the world, it is not imperfect and does not need to be amended to meet the changing conditions and times. When we apply the Word of God that is contained in every verse of the Bible, it becomes a sword of excellence in our hands to execute God's will in our lives.

When we learn the precepts and principles contained in the Word and apply them to the judgment of people and affairs in our lives, we exercise the power of judgment

6. God Governance is Good Governance

of God. We are the Viceroys of God on earth. When we place our trust in the Lord and His justice, He shares His power with us. I heard an amazing prophecy from a nun who was called by the Lord out of the convent in which she served as a principal. She said that one day as she was praying, the Lord revealed that He had appointed me as a watchman for the nation and that He had placed the legislature, executive and judiciary in my hands. That revelation is not exclusive to me alone but to every believer. As we watch and observe things happening in our nations, the Lord gives us the power to influence or bring about changes even in the governance of the country. We can pray for the removal of corrupt or despotic or misguided members of the ruling class in every nation.

As diligent rulers on behalf of God, we must not neglect to observe the details of events happening around us but after taking note of the details bring it to the Lord's throne of judgment and mercy in prayer and faith. Everything happens first in the spirit world before it happens in our world. He will also save us from the corrupt, despotic or misguided ways of people in position and power. The latter might think that they cannot be questioned but the Lord is the arbiter of their destiny. We might think that we are helpless against persons and people in position, power or influence, but, the Lord puts His strength and power on the side of the weak against the strong. Indeed, God's governance leads to good governance.

7. THE TRANSMISSION

"JOSHUA THE SON OF NUN WAS FULL OF THE SPIRIT OF WISDOM, FOR MOSES HAD LAID HIS HANDS UPON HIM AND THE CHILDREN OF ISRAEL HEARKENED UNTO HIM AND DID AS THE LORD COMMANDED MOSES."

– **Deuteronomy 34:9**

During a time of prayer, the Lord promised to give us the authority of Joshua. The Holy Spirit revealed the difference between the leadership of Moses and the leadership of Joshua. No one murmured against Joshua while they murmured against Moses. Yet, it was the laying of the hands of Moses upon Joshua that led to the transmission of the spirit of wisdom to the latter. It was on account of this anointing of the Holy Spirit, the Spirit of wisdom, that the people of Israel listened to him and obeyed the commandments the Lord gave through Moses.

There is a series of cause-and-effect sequences in this uni-verse. Moses laid his hands upon Joshua as directed by the Lord. Joshua was filled with the spirit of wisdom. The Israelites listened to him without murmuring, they obeyed the commandments of the Lord. The transmission of wisdom should precede the assumption and exercise of authority. In the early church, too when the apostles laid hands upon the people and prayed they were filled with

7. The Transmission

the Holy Spirit. The anointing, the authority and the spirit of wisdom are the basis of godly or spiritual leadership. It is transmitted through the laying of hands though it is not the only means. We must be careful who we ask to lay their hands upon us to pray. We need to discern if they have the anointing themselves: do they speak with God face to face like Moses? In other words, do they relate and communicate directly with the Lord? We need to discern their gifts and the fruit of the spirit manifesting in their lives.

The mere laying of hands that is not backed by a life lived in a close fellowship with the Trinity would be in vain, an empty gesture. As believers, we all have traces of wisdom but we need to be filled with the spirit of wisdom. We need to be saturated with godly wisdom so that it overflows into our decisions, actions, reactions, relationships, leadership, professions and lives. The scripture also warns that we must not lay hands on other people in haste. We must discern their hearts and their motives. In the early church, Simon wanted the apostles to lay their hands on him so that he could profit monetarily by laying his hands upon others. It should also not turn into a cultic practice where certain teachers even virtually sell physical objects and symbols for specific sums or donations in order to raise money for their projects. Such practices in the contemporary church need to be condemned by one and all and seen for what it is, it does not come from God. The transmission is meant to fulfil a God-given mission and not to turn it into a money-making machine.

8. SHINING STARS IN GOD'S KINGDOM

"THEY THAT BE WISE SHALL SHINE AS THE BRIGHTNESS OF THE FIRMAMENT AND THEY THAT TURN MANY TO RIGHTEOUSNESS AS THE STARS FOREVER AND EVER."

– **Daniel 12:3**

One morning at the break of dawn as I walked, prayed and meditated in our garden, the stars, the moon and some planets shone brightly in the sky. The Lord reminded me of this uni-verse where the wise, those who fear God, repent of their sin and accept the remission of sins through Christ, will shine as the brightness of the heavens. They have no light of their own- the planets and satellites that do not shine as bright as the stars that have the light of their own. They merely reflect the light of other heavenly bodies. Having repented and received salvation, they will further turn many to fear God and do likewise. When we lead others to God through Christ, we shine even more brightly as the stars. We will have the light of our own, our own spheres of influence and leadership.

The stars in the ancient world were the only signposts that helped sailors and travellers navigate and find their way around. Similarly, believers are the lodestars that

8. Shining Stars In God's Kingdom

guide people into truth and a relationship with God. The powerful emperors under whom Daniel, a former slave who rose in rank by dint of God's grace and his integrity, worked were soon forgotten. Their mighty and extensive empires too vanished into thin air as if they never existed. Daniel was wise while they were otherwise. Daniel's name continues to inspire faith and righteous living to this day. His fear of God and his willingness to risk all for the sake of his faith in God made him shine brightly as the heavens. His encouraging his companions to remain steadfast in their faith, his testimony of how he interpreted the dreams of kings and his writing down the awesome prophecies he received in visions further made him shine as a star.

He remains a shining star of God's Kingdom that lasts forever. He could have chosen the path of least resistance as many do in government service, but, he chose the more risky and more difficult option. Just as a star has a gravitational pull, we will attract many people to the light that is in us. We need to be a shepherd to many lost souls, to impart to them that which we have learnt from God's Word and that which we have experienced in accordance with God's Word to convince, persuade, warn, teach, explain, train and mentor others in the dynamics of the Kingdom of God. According to this uni-verse, there are only two kinds of people, the wise and the otherwise. We need to make the choice.

9. THE STANDARDS OF THE LORD

"THE LORD SAID UNTO SAMUEL, 'LOOK NOT ON HIS COUNTENANCE OR THE HEIGHT OF HIS STATURE, BECAUSE I HAVE REFUSED HIM, FOR THE LORD SEETH NOT AS MAN SEETH FOR MAN LOOKETH ON THE OUTWARD APPEARANCE, BUT THE LORD LOOKETH ON THE HEART.'"

– **I Samuel 16:7**

*H*uman standards are distinct and different from the standards of our Lord and God. This is the precise reason why mankind can never work out our salvation ourselves by good deeds or repentance or karma. It is written that what is highly esteemed by men is an abomination in the sight of God. Our eyes of flesh are covetous and idolatrous. We desire what we see and we desire what is good to look at, what is glamourous and beautiful on the exterior. We are keen on the packaging and not the content. Huge crowds of people in India and other countries adore their cricketing stars, not just for their batting prowess but because they seem "macho" and good to look at. You will find even in the choir of a church, the good-looking ones will be put on the frontline! Our eyes of flesh are superficial-we judge and decide many things on the basis of cosmetic appearance. Instead, we need to decide and

9. The Standards of the Lord

choose people on the basis of their thoughts, inclinations and intentions.

The scripture interestingly uses the word "reins" – we need to choose people on the basis of their inner controls that restrain them from the negatives and motivators that egg them on towards positives. The first time around Samuel was directed by the Lord to choose and anoint a king for Israel, he went by the stature of the nominee. He found Saul to be head and shoulders above the rest of Israel. It qualified him to be king in the eyes of Samuel the prophet, but, the next time, the Lord directed him not to go by the comely appearance or the stature.

These first seven sons of Jesse were fighting men, soldiers in Saul's army. Even their profession or prowess did not qualify them. Samuel could not look into the hearts of the sons of Jesse. The Lord looks into the hearts of people. He is interested primarily in emotional engagement with people. He sees the inmost mind or the innermost desires and longings of the human heart. He discerns our priorities in life. By this criterion, He chooses, anoints and reveals His mind and will to these chosen vessels to perform His special tasks. A comely appearance while it does not qualify a person for the mantle of leadership in God's eyes, it also does not disqualify him or her. David who was summoned as an afterthought from the fields where he tended the sheep was good-looking and handsome. Yet, the Lord told Samuel, "Arise, anoint him for this is he."

The Lord had looked into his heart even as he tended the sheep and saw a heart that was always emotionally engaged with Him: a constant love dialogue running in his heart and mind, praising God for the stars and all that was fearfully and wonderfully made by His hands. Today's corporates and human resource managers can pick a page from Samuel's experience: when we recruit people or assign leadership roles, ask the Lord to help us discern the person's heart as He alone can. In the New Testament times that we now live in, we can ask for the gift of the Holy Spirit, the gift of discernment that will help us discern not just the hearts but also the spirit of the person. The unique thing about the human heart is that it does not remain the same but can change with changed circumstances. We see what success and victory did to David's heart- in a weak moment, he yielded to the temptation of adultery followed by vicarious murder. The heart needs to be guarded diligently throughout a lifetime.

10. THE ROYAL PRIESTHOOD

"HE HATH MADE US KINGS AND PRIESTS UNTO GOD AND HIS FATHER, TO HIM BE GLORY AND DOMINION FOREVER AND EVER. AMEN."

– **Revelations 1:6**

Christ by His sacrificial death on the cross of Calvary purchased for us with His blood salvation or eternal life, implying that we will not be subject to a second spiritual death after our spirits depart from our physical bodies, but, not just that He has made us kings and priests or part of a royal priesthood in the order of Melchizedek. We are not born kings and priests but He has made us so. Hence, we derive our authority from the Lord. We must always remain accountable and thankful to Him for the exercise of godly authority and priestly office. As kings, we have authority over all rulers and princes of darkness. We can wage spiritual warfare to claim back souls and to extend the dominion of God.

Melchizedek was paid a tribute by Abraham. Similarly, we will eat the fruits of the Gentiles or unbelievers. People in position and power will tremble and fear when they encounter us as they see God's inner power at work in us. He has called us from the spiritual darkness or blindness of this world into the light or full vision of His glory. As kings, we must make plans for the extension of God's authority and power in the areas of our influence. As priests, we must lead sanctified or pure lives. As priests, we must offer prayers and worship on behalf of all the people we know who do not yet know, understand or believe Him. As kings, we execute the will of God on earth. As priests, we are His ministers to serve Him in all our ways. We can stand in the gap pleading and interceding for nations or the rest of humanity. The Lord will not remain deaf or mute as we plead with Him. He will send His angels, His spirit servants and even His servants in flesh and blood, believers to help us, to facilitate our work or to fructify our plans.

As kings, we need to be firm in the exercise of power and authority but as priests, we need to be meek, compassionate, understanding and patient. The Holy Spirit once affirmed to me through the words of a prophet, "You know how to handle authority with humility and firmness." Once I read in the paper that an astrologer predicted big disasters throughout the world in a particular year. I prayed not just cancelling the power of that prediction, I prayed for that particular astrologer. The latter and his wife saw and testified to seeing a vision of Jesus. As kings, we need to pass decrees by mingling our prayers with the Word of God declaring and proclaiming victory over every power of darkness. Then, the Lord will ordain and order even the forces of nature to work to help us or assist us in our tasks. Many leaders try to echo the thoughts of new-age philosophers who say that when we are pursuing a particular purpose, even the universe will conspire to create circumstances favourable to us. This is a myth. The universe is as inert as a piece of wood or iron.

10. The Royal Priesthood

It is the Creator of the Universe who ordains and orders our circumstances. All glory and dominion are meant not for the creation but for the Creator, the Father of lights.

11. LEADERSHIP BY PROMISE

"HAVE I NOT COMMANDED YOU? BE STRONG AND COURAGEOUS. DO NOT BE AFRAID; DO NOT BE DISCOURAGED, FOR THE LORD YOUR GOD WILL BE WITH YOU WHEREVER YOU GO."

– Joshua 1 V 9

*T*his uni-verse is a fantastic promise of the Lord. It pays to pay attention to the Word. He promises to make us the head or the commander, the leader, the chief, the Numero Uno, the pioneer, the premier, the trendsetter and the pacesetter. Some become leaders owing to situations, some others owing to birth and some others due to their talents and skills. These are market leaders while we are "marked leaders." For we are leaders by fulfilment of this promise. The conditions, of course, apply: We need to pay attention to the commands of the Lord our God. In other words, we need to pay attention to the Word of God. Paying attention means to be absorbed in, to incline our ears to hear the Word, to apply our minds to understand it, to use our hearts to store it, to employ our spirits to pray or breathe it in and to focus our wills to decide on the basis of the Word.

The Lord gives us commands this day and every day. There are commands specific to this particular day that we need to carefully follow. We need to diligently study

11. Leadership By Promise

these commands and walk carefully in the path indicated. To follow carefully implies we need to obey in letter and spirit the Word of God, taking care not to violate the will of God in the matter indicated to us this day. We must do it not out of a sense of duty or obligation but with a sense of delight. We must not obey His commands grudgingly or unwillingly but wholeheartedly and with pleasure. We will be leaders in due time and the manner decided by the Lord. We need to not only pay attention but also pray for the ability and grace to be attentive and obedient to the Word. Only those who are led by the Spirit of God can and should lead or else we will be like the blind leading the blind. We will not know where we are and where we are heading.

The first sign or symptom of a head or leader is that he or she has a sense of direction and a vision for himself or herself and the ones who follow him or her. The second mark of leadership is that he or she cares enough for God to pay attention to His Word or commands. The values that are contained in the Word will get impregnated in the leader's character. He takes us through a process to make this happen. Now, we are ready for leadership. We will always be at the top and never at the bottom. The world or even our family or colleagues may not recognise that we are at the top but the Lord recognises our leadership brand. Joseph was not recognised as a leader by his father and brothers, by his fellow slaves or fellow prisoners. Yet, he was the one marked to be the leader. He was the one with the multi-coloured coat.

Joseph was the one whom God chose to visit with dreams or a vision for his life. He was the one Potiphar relied upon. He was the one whom the prison head trusted. He was the one in whom his fellow prisoners confided their dreams. He was the one who interpreted Pharaoh's dream. He was the one who led Egypt through the years of plenty and years of famine. Like Joseph, we are given a dream or vision for our lives. We are given a multi-coloured coat or multi-talented or multi-gifted personalities. Even when we are at the bottom of a pit on a particular day or phase in our lives, we are in God's eyes always at the top.

12. INTEGRITY OF HEART

"SO HE FED THEM ACCORDING TO THE INTEGRITY OF HIS HEART AND GUIDED THEM BY THE SKILLFULNESS OF HIS HANDS."

– **Psalms 78:72**

David as a shepherd led his sheep faithfully and diligently to the extent that he staked his life to save them from a lion's jaws. This was a time of preparation and grooming for him to lead the nation of Israel. He fed the sheep from the pastures on the hills surrounding his home but he fed Israel from the Word he received from the Lord. He was true to the Word except in the matter of his adultery with Bathsheba and her husband Uriah, the Hittite. He truly repented from his heart for that fall from grace when he acted in the flesh and fell to temptation. He humbled himself before God and did not deny his sin. The Lord, therefore, certified that David is a man after his own heart who did His will. The integrity of heart or oneness with the heart of the Lord comes from hearing the voice of the one true Shepherd, Jesus and obeying His Word in our lives.

It is reflected in all that we think, feel, speak and do. It is reflected in our relationships. It is reflected in our professional work. David desired with all his heart to please the Lord and therefore though he desired to build the temple of the Lord, he passed on that responsibility to his son Solomon as directed by the Spirit of the Lord. The integrity of the heart requires us to discern the feelings of the Lord and to act accordingly. Once our hearts are aligned with the Lord, His Word and His will, we will have wisdom, knowledge, understanding and insight or the skills of leadership that enable us to guide others to the Lord. The Lord will use us to counsel and mentor others in His ways. Leadership that depends too much on skills or charisma or communication tends to fail. Integrity is the first attribute that should be in place. As someone said, "With integrity in place, nothing else matters. Without it in place, nothing else matters."

13. SPIRITUAL AUTHORITY

"SO HE SAID TO ME, 'THIS IS THE WORD OF THE LORD TO ZERUBBABEL, NOT BY MIGHT, NOR BY POWER, BUT BY MY SPIRIT,' SAYS THE LORD ALMIGHTY."

– **Zechariah 4:6**

The Spirit that the Lord imparts to us when we believe in His Word rests or remains on us and in us, renewing us as His new creation or re-creation. He gives us the self-same Spirit that rested on Jesus, the Spirit of wisdom and understanding, the Spirit of counsel and power, the Spirit of knowledge and the fear of the Lord. We will delight in the fear of the Lord, implying we will delight in His Word and its obedience. We will not judge anymore by what we see with our eyes or decide by what we hear by our ears. We will not rely on our physical and intellectual senses but will depend on the insight that the Lord gives us and the promptings of the Holy Spirit. Righteousness, justice and faithfulness are the hallmarks of our lives. The Word that the Lord quickens to our spirit is mightier than swords, spears, horses, chariots, aircraft, ships or nuclear bombs. What the Lord speaks, He then performs. The Lord will speak to individuals specifically as He spoke a specific Word to Zerubbabel, a governor who hailed from the royal lineage of King David.

Each believer is a Zerubbabel in God's eyes and His purpose for us to build the new covenant temple, the residence of the Lord in our own bodies, minds and spirits. If He has spoken a word of healing, He will cause it to happen in due time. If He has spoken a word of deliverance, He will deliver whether it is from all the strongholds of spiritual darkness or earthly powers or mighty rulers or the jaws of death. The Word of God or Jesus is the ultimate arbiter of law on earth. He will slay the wicked, the unrepentant and those who do not show any sign of respect or reverence or fear of God with the breath of His lips. In the time of Moses, the Lord God had revealed His mighty power by delivering with His outstretched right arm of power (or through an open manifestation of His power and might) the Jewish nation from slavery and bondage in Egypt, but this uni-verse is a watershed for the Lord is declaring that in these last days from the beginning of the new covenant, His modus operandi would be to rely on the Spirit-led Word to fulfil His plan and purpose for His people or the believers in Christ.

Our weapons of warfare, namely the Word and praying in the spirit are more powerful and effective in pulling down spiritual strongholds of evil and darkness. By these means, we will be able to cast down every imagination and every high thing that exalts itself against the knowledge of God and bring into captivity every thought to the obedience of Christ. It is not through political or military or economic power or religious fervour or social upheaval that lasting change will be brought about but by the power of God manifested in a gentle, quiet and patient way through the

13. Spiritual Authority

ministry of the Holy Spirit. The Holy Spirit will convict people with the Word of God and establish the Kingdom of God on earth. The Lord has given us spiritual authority over every physical, intellectual, emotional and spiritual realm on the earth. Authority implies legitimate power that is exercised in accordance with the written Word. This uni-verse is an invitation for us to partner with the Lord in the exercise of our spiritual authority and so usher in His rule in our lives and the lives of others around us.

14. ANOINTED TO SERVE

"THEN HE SAID TO ME, 'THESE TWO ARE THE ONES ANOINTED TO SERVE THE LORD OF ALL THE EARTH.'"

– Zechariah 4:14

*T*he two olive trees that stand next to the seven lamps that are connected by seven golden pipes to the golden bowl on top are the believers who are connected to the Lord all the time. Kings and priests were anointed with oil to serve God and people from biblical times. It was a sign to others and themselves that they were chosen, sanctified and enabled to serve, but under the new covenant, believers are anointed by the Holy Spirit to serve as a royal priesthood or in the dual role of kings and priests. To be anointed to serve the Lord of all the earth is a higher calling than to be a mere mortal king or leader or priest. To be anointed means to be divinely enabled to perform this role of representing God before people and people before God.

The functions to be performed in the course of such service of the Lord are to proclaim the good news to the spiritually repentant or poor, to heal broken hearts and to set spiritual captives free from bondages of darkness. We are priests forever and kings forever in the order of Melchizedek, the King and High Priest of Salem. The two olive trees in the above uni-verse represented the ruler

Zerubbabel, a descendant of David and Joshua, the priest. Each believer today is called to be a descendant of David who is to exercise royal authority over the spiritual realms and a priest to intercede for people. First of all, we are to play this dual role inside our own homes, but, the Lord has not set any boundaries in heaven or on earth to exercise our authority and our priestly function. One man can stand in the gap before the Lord on behalf of nations to turn away His wrath from them.

Another meaning is that couples or husband and wife together perform this role. They are to act as olive trees before the Lord. An olive tree's fruit is useful and when crushed is full of oil. We too must be full of the anointing of the Holy Spirit. We should seek the fruit of the Spirit more eagerly than even the gifts of the Spirit. We must be faithful in the exercise of our various spiritual gifts on behalf of the church or to build and encourage the body of believers. Like an olive tree that lives on for a long time, we too must have an enduring legacy to leave behind us. The branches of the olive tree dipping into the oil of the lamps imply that our thoughts and emotions should be always immersed in understanding and rejoicing in the Word and prayer. Regardless of what the rest of the world thinks or the price we have to pay, our attitude should be that of Joshua, "As for me and my household, we shall serve the Lord."

15. THREE FUNCTIONS, ONE PURPOSE

"FOR THE LORD IS OUR JUDGE, THE LORD IS OUR LAWGIVER, THE LORD IS OUR KING, HE WILL SAVE US."

– **Isaiah 33:22**

We all know that the government consists of the executive, the head, the legislature, the law-making wing and the judiciary, the judge. Long before such institutions were set up as the three separate branches of government, the Word indicated this functional division, but the Lord combines in Himself the functions and positions of the judge, lawgiver and king. As a Judge, His chief qualities are His justice and mercy. As a lawgiver, His chief qualities are His wisdom, knowledge and understanding. As a King, His chief qualities are His graciousness, majesty and power to execute His will. He is also the lone author of eternal salvation. He uses His good offices of judge, lawgiver and king to save us. As a Judge, He shows us mercy on the basis of our faith in Jesus. He justifies us or sets us right with God as if we have never fallen short of His law or justice as if we have never sinned.

As a lawgiver, He gives us His Word to guide and lead us, to comfort, strengthen and nourish us. As a King He

15. Three Functions, One Purpose

commands His deliverances for us. He rewards us for our faithfulness. In all three roles and functions, His chief goal or priority is to save us. The justice, law and power of God are tailored for our salvation, not for our condemnation. Whatever our shortcomings in every area of life, He shows us mercy and gives us the grace to overcome. He removes earthly kings and installs new ones in their place. He weighs every leader and authority, measures them and numbers their days. There is no conflict between the executive, legislative and judicial functions of God, unlike our human institutions which are often at loggerheads with each other.

We can be confident and trust the Lord that He never errs in His judgments. His statutes and decrees are also wise, perfect and trustworthy. In His executive function, the Lord acts consistent with His law. His decrees or decisions based on His law are what operate in our lives. What is impossible for man is only improbable for God. He takes a decision and the impossible happens. As merciful Judges, we need to trust Him. As wise lawgivers, we need to respect the law we have received at the mouth of God, the Word. As an all-powerful King, we need to be loyal, faithful and obedient. The uni-verse states that the Lord has three supreme functions but only one purpose in mind, the salvation of those who trust, revere and depend on Him. The word "is", is repeated thrice to emphasise that we need to know Him as a Judge, Lawgiver, King and Saviour in this lifetime and not just as a future King or Judge or Lawgiver.

16. FEED LIKE A SHEPHERD, GRAZE LIKE THE SHEEP

"HE SAITH UNTO HIM THE THIRD TIME, 'SIMON, SON OF JONAS, LOVEST THOU ME?' PETER WAS GRIEVED BECAUSE HE SAID UNTO HIM THE THIRD TIME, 'LOVEST THOU ME?' HE SAID UNTO HIM, 'LORD, THOU KNOWEST ALL THINGS, THOU KNOWEST THAT I LOVE THEE.' JESUS SAITH UNTO HIM, 'FEED MY SHEEP.'"

– John 21:17

Peter denied Christ thrice before His trial and crucifixion but he also affirmed the risen Christ thrice after His resurrection and just before His ascension to Heaven. He affirmed that he loved Jesus. Peter was hurt that Jesus asked him thrice, but the purpose was to annul the three denials that Peter made. Satan could no longer accuse him of having said that he did not know the man Jesus and had nothing to do with Him. We might have denied Jesus a thousand times but our affirmations and confessions of faith will cancel the weight and consequences of the denials. Up till this point, Jesus had been playing the role of the Good Shepherd who fed His sheep.

By asking the same question thrice, He was preparing Peter to take on that role to feed the disciples and believers.

16. Feed Like A Shepherd, Graze Like the Sheep

"To feed the sheep," meant to encourage, guide, admonish, inspire, teach, minister, explain, illustrate, declare and demonstrate in practical and real ways. Jesus rarely repeated His golden Words for He is a person of perfect speech and perfect wisdom. Yet, why did He choose to ask Peter the same question thrice? Jesus is driving home not just to Peter but to all humanity that the greatest task of leadership is not to lead but to feed, to feed not our egos but those who follow Him. Peter was commissioned for the task of leadership, to feed the other apostles as well as disciples, followers and believers of the time with the Words of eternal life that He Himself had taught him.

We feed others around us with spiritual nourishment when we teach them the Word and when we share our experiences of the love, grace and mercy of God. When we love the Word of God, it is the surest sign that we love God with all our heart, soul and mind. When we satisfy the longing for truth and meaning, the searching, the spiritual hunger and thirst of people of our generation, we are fulfilling the highest calling or purpose to which the Lord has called us. Through this uni-verse series of meditations, the Lord has called me to feed His sheep in different parts of the world. It will augment their faith, answer unanswered questions, ignite faith in new areas, increase their maturity and release the wisdom and power of God in their lives. I am also being fed spiritual food at the same time. Just as a water tank has water flowing into it and then flowing out of it to many outlets, we need to be a reservoir for the Lord. In terms of the frequency of feeding, we ought to be like the sheep. The sheep do not just graze and feed thrice or four times a day but they are grazing wherever and whenever they find pasture. If they are not grazing, they are chewing. Similarly, we need to be feeding as frequently as possible and in between those times of feeding, we should be chewing or meditating on what we had read or heard.

The leadership and management concept derived from this uni-verse is that the chief function of leadership is feeding the sheep and not leading per se. Most of the time the leaders of this world are wolves who feed on the sheep and instead of meeting the spiritual and other needs of the sheep are using the sheep to feed their needs. The principles evolved from this concept are: a) Our love for God is reflected in how and how much we are involved in feeding His people b) The more the sheep are fed, the quicker they turn into shepherds. The practical steps that we can take to translate these principles into practice are 1.) Set aside time in our daily schedules to feed on the Word 2.) Set aside time in our weekly or monthly schedules to feed the believers with spiritual food or the Word.

17. A GOOD SOLDIER OF JESUS

"THOU THEREFORE ENDURE HARDNESS, AS A GOOD SOLDIER OF JESUS CHRIST."

– 2 Timothy 2:3

A good soldier endures hardship. He is used to a hard life, to travel at short notice, to be called to fight in a war he never started. He is loyal to his commanding officer. He is obedient and respectful. He would give his life for his commander and his nation. His life in fact is always at stake. He keeps himself fit physically and mentally. He is constantly in training towards this end. He is focused on victory for his side. He knows that strategy is as important as strength in fighting to win. He does not waste his blows or indulges in shadowboxing. He is not involved in civilian affairs. His loyalty cannot be purchased with bribes or allurement.

A good soldier is well-equipped for every type of contingency. He wears his whole body armour to protect himself from head to foot. He carries his personal weapon. Similarly, a good soldier of Jesus needs to exhibit all these qualities and adopt all these habits. He should understand the mind of Christ, His commander. He will not give any quarter to the enemy to compromise the security of the wider army he belongs to. He trusts his commander that He is invincible, that neither sin nor satan nor death could defeat him. Sin, satan and death had defeated virtually every other commander of any army in human history. A good soldier of Christ knows that most of his battles would be won as he spends time on his knees.

A soldier of Christ will help to recruit and train other followers. His goal is the goal that Christ has set, the salvation of every human soul. He will not develop habits that will weaken him. Rather, he will develop habits that will strengthen him physically, emotionally, spiritually, intellectually and socially. He will keep his s-word, the Word always unsheathed in his heart and mind. He will draw his strength therefrom to do whatever the commander bids him. He will be prepared to face grave risks and threats to his life but at the same time, he will not be foolhardy or tactless or naïve. He will claim ultimate and immediate victory based on the promises of God. A good soldier knows when to make strategic advances and when to make tactical retreats. A good soldier knows the terrain as well as the people he would be dealing with. He is practical and never takes leave of his senses. A good soldier would be stern and strict as well as humble and willing to learn from the humblest of human beings. Naaman, the Syrian general was a good soldier. Despite having a formidable reputation as a general and the confidence of the king, he was willing to listen to the counsel of a maid to seek healing for his leprosy. A good soldier would know where to seek remedy for his afflictions. He knows how best to use the resources available to him. He never lets down his guard and is always watchful and alert.

18. USING THE AUTHORITY OF THE AUTHOR

"SEE, I HAVE THIS DAY SET THEE OVER THE NATIONS AND OVER THE KINGDOMS, TO ROOT OUT AND TO PULL DOWN AND TO DESTROY AND TO THROW DOWN, TO BUILD AND TO PLANT."

– Jeremiah 1:10

We should not just read the scripture but we should see that which is promised as if it is already real and happening. Belief is the equivalent of what knowledge is in the seen world. We see only that which our minds know. We should know that God has set us over nations and all kingdoms. We should see ourselves set up as spiritual leaders over the nations and the kingdoms. The Lord has set us up to root out or uproot spiritual kingdoms and principalities of darkness. He has given us spiritual authority and weapons to pull down and to destroy strongholds. We are to uproot evil and plant goodness, overcome wickedness and build the strongholds of the Lord.

Everything happens first in the spiritual world and then it gets reflected in our physical world. We exercise our authority to break curses and heal diseases and relationships. The word "authority" comes from the author. A person becomes an author when he or she has mastery of a particular subject or topic. Jesus is the author and finisher of our faith. He is also the author of life. The rules and principles of the seen and the unseen worlds, of heaven and the earth, are all written in the Word. Jesus has delegated His authority to us who believe. We can consult Jesus in all matters of faith and life and He will give us discernment about what we have to root out of our own lives, what we have to pull down in our lives, what to destroy and throw away and what to build and plant. Our faith needs to be built and the Word of God that is the good seed has to be planted in our hearts.

We need to pray in the Spirit and the Spirit will establish and build us up. He will also uproot that which has to be eradicated in our own lives as well as in society, be it evil, traditions, poverty, violence or terrorism. The Spirit will also plant us in good soil and nourish us so that we bear good fruit in season and out of season. We ourselves need to be rooted in the Lord, the Spirit and the Word just as the teeth are rooted in the gums. When we are so rooted, He will give us power over all the power of the enemy. He has given us kingly power to root out, to pull down strongholds, to destroy and throw down. He has given us priestly power to build, to bless, to plant. We need to align our plans, thoughts, temperament, tongues, talent and time with the revealed will of the Lord. When we live and act according to the plan of God for our lives, we become a plant for Him to manifest His love and splendour.

19. STEWARDSHIP OF LEADER GIFTS

"HE THAT EXHORTETH, ON EXHORTATION, HE THAT GIVETH, LET HIM DO IT WITH SIMPLICITY, HE THAT RULETH, WITH DILIGENCE, HE THAT SHEWETH MERCY, WITH CHEERFULNESS."

– **Romans 12:8**

The grace of God is manifold and He distributes gifts liberally to His chosen ones in order that these gifts be exercised for the benefit of all, to build relationships of people with God and to transform character, conduct and communication. Many think that leadership is an art that can be learnt. This uni-verse states that leadership or authority to lead is itself a spiritual gift or calling from God to be exercised with more than just due diligence but extraordinary diligence. According to our calling, we are given appropriate gifts that we should discover, own, use, develop, manage and give glory to God. We are to be good stewards of the gifts given to us.

Leaders or rulers or administrators are to rule or act with diligence. Diligence implies that one needs to study every aspect of the assigned work rigourously. We need to analyse, understand and apply ourselves to the task at hand. We ought not to conform to the patterns of leadership in the world but be transformed by renewing our minds with the continual study of the patterns of leadership contained in the Word. We are called to be first transformed before we can ourselves be agents of transformation.

In the world, many people exhort in order to extort, but the Lord expects godly leaders to exhort people to encourage them to grow to the very stature of Christ. In the world, many people give in order to build their reputation or with some other motive, but the Lord wants us to give with liberality and without publicity. We are also called to show mercy to others for wilful acts or accidental errors even as the Lord is merciful to us. It also implies that we show compassion to those who are hurting in their lives.

20. THE DEW OF LEADERSHIP

"GOD DID SO THAT NIGHT, FOR IT WAS DRY UPON THE FLEECE ONLY AND THERE WAS DEW ON ALL THE GROUND."

– Judges 6:40

Gideon wanted a sign of confirmation from God that He would save Israel from the powerful Midianites through his leadership. The first time he asked that the fleece of wool would be wet with dew and the ground all around dry. He could wring a bowlful of water when he squeezed the fleece. He sought another sign, this time he asked that the fleece would be dry but on all the ground around there would be dew. After this double confirmation, Gideon had no more doubt that God would deliver the Midianites into his hands. He was so full of faith that he went against the Midianite army with just a force of 300 armed only with trumpets and earthen jars and each carrying a burning torch within a jar.

Gideon remembered the testimony of his forefathers of how Jehovah had done mighty miracles that led to the deliverance of the Jewish nations from the bondage of Egypt. He knew that God was capable of delivering Israel as He had done before but he only wanted to confirm and be sure that he was the one chosen to lead, the one who is anointed by Almighty God with His power. Similarly, in our struggles and battles, we too can seek a sign of confirmation from the Lord. I once asked for a sign of His favour and He showed me several signs in the form of seven rainbows over several months. The Lord knows we are human, that we are weak in faith and that we can be filled with doubt and discouragement at times.

He knows that we are often bewildered by the odds against us. He is willing to give us a sign. He is willing even to give another sign to confirm that the sign He gave is indeed from Him and not a mere fluke or accident. Hezekiah was another king who sought a miraculous sign of God's favour. He asked that the light on the sundial move forward and then he asked that it move back a few degrees. Both Gideon and Hezekiah did not ask for a sign from God casually but with great reverence. We must not ask for a sign in order to test God but only to find encouragement and strength. When the spirit of leaders around the world is dry, the Lord will send the dew of His grace, love, power and compassion upon His chosen vessels. He will give us a bowlful to drink and to be strengthened in the spirit that we go forth and lead more and more people to victory and joy in life. As the scripture says, "The tender mercies of the Lord are fresh every morning." He gives us a fresh anointing with the dew of His anointing every morning to face the challenges of the day and end it victoriously. The word "dew" stands for a combination of determination, energy and wisdom. He will give us the determination, energy or enthusiasm and wisdom to be godly leaders in this generation, to wrest great victories for His glory.

21. THE TEST OF GOOD AND GODLY LEADERSHIP

"IT CAME TO PASS, THAT ON THE MORROW MOSES WENT INTO THE TABERNACLE OF WITNESS AND BEHOLD, THE ROD OF AARON FOR THE HOUSE OF LEVI WAS BUDDED AND BROUGHT FORTH BUDS AND BLOOMED BLOSSOMS AND YIELDED ALMONDS."

– **Numbers 17:8**

When all of Israel rebelled against the leadership of Moses and questioned the priestly calling of Aaron, Moses conducted the litmus test of spiritual and wholesome leadership in an amazing miracle that is also a parable for all time. Moses asked the twelve chiefs or leaders of Israel including Aaron to bring their sceptre, a dried rod of the almond tree, to him. Moses placed the twelve rods each with the respective names of Aaron and the other leaders. He left the twelve rods in the Tabernacle of the Lord's presence overnight. The next morning when he entered the tent, he found only Aaron's rod had budded, blossomed and bore leaves and fruit of almonds on the dry stick proving that Aaron alone was chosen by God to be a priest to serve Him and bear fruit for the Kingdom of God.

The dry stick of Aaron bore buds, blossoms of flowers and fruits as well as leaves, all three appearing at the same time on the same rod against the course of nature proving that it was a sure sign from God confirming the priestly calling of Aaron. Moses had prophesied that this would happen before he asked the leaders to submit to this test. This put an end to all time the murmuring of the people. By not submitting to the leadership of Moses and Aaron, the people of Israel brought death upon themselves. It was a warning for all time not to rebel or complain or murmur against God-anointed leaders.

If we are watchful, prayerful and worshipful, the Lord will make our lives and our leadership fruitful and blessed in both natural and supernatural ways. He will cause both our leaves or our thoughts, our words, our hopes, our buds or our ideas, plans, projects, visions to grow and our flowers to blossom or the things that make our lives beautiful and fragrant, our almonds, fruits or results, achievements, contributions to be enduring and amazing. The lesson from this parable-miracle is that godly leaders will not just be outstanding but astounding in the impact and fruitfulness of their lives. When we spend time in the presence of the Lord, soaking in His grace, glorious things will happen to confirm that we are truly led by the Lord. The Lord will hasten or quicken even what is dead and dry in our lives to give a fitting reply to those who question our credentials, those who murmur, envy, rebel, accuse, place obstacles or hinder in any way.

The Lord will make our thoughts and words the leaves of the sceptre of leadership, our intentions, desires,

21. The Test of Good and Godly Leadership

goals and plans the buds, our acts of goodness, faith and grace the flowers and our effects, impact, legacy and work the fruits. When we had a time of prayer in the Tabernacle, our home, the Lord said, "Your father was like Aaron's dry stick but it has now budded, blossomed and borne leaves and fruit in the form of two brothers who serve the Lord." The true source of effective leadership, the only source of the authority of both kings and priests is God Himself. Only those who truly follow God can be true leaders, priests and kings.

22. BEING A SERVANT LEADER, NOT A SERPENT LEADER

"GOD BLESSED THEM AND GOD SAID UNTO THEM, 'BE FRUITFUL, MULTIPLY AND REPLENISH THE EARTH AND SUBDUE IT AND HAVE DOMINION OVER THE FISH OF THE SEA, OVER THE FOWL OF THE AIR AND OVER EVERY LIVING THING THAT MOVETH UPON THE EARTH.'"

– **Genesis 1:28**

This uni-verse speaks of what God had in mind when He created mankind. It speaks of six phenomena that together constitute the purpose of human life, "blessing," being "fruitful," multiplication, replenishment, subduing and having dominion. It is not success that we should seek in life but to be blessed by God. Success could be one of the blessings of the Lord. We are called to be fruitful not just physically like other creatures but intellectually and spiritually. The ultimate fruit of life that we need to abound in are the fruit of the spirit: love, joy, peace, patience, kindness, goodness, faithfulness, humility and self-control. Wisdom is the eclectic quality that binds and balances all these fruit together in one person. We are called to multiply our talents, by using known abilities

22. Being a Servant Leader, Not a Serpent Leader

and gifts and discovering new ones that we never suspected we ever had.

We are called to replenish the earth, implying that we are not just to be consumers but people who contribute to making the world a better place in small or big ways. We are to be a blessing to others by sharing their burdens and trying to lighten them. We got to subdue what needs to be subdued. We need to subdue the evil within us and around us. We are given the spiritual authority to subdue, rebuke and command every wickedness in high places. Finally, we are given the authority to dominate, lead, influence, teach, to be an example. Adam and Eve forfeited their right to lead and dominate by allowing the serpent to lead and dominate them. Most of the time throughout history we have had "serpent leadership" or leadership that attempts to influence through a mixture of good and evil, through subtlety, suggestion, cunning, deceit and duplicity.

A serpent leader misleads, misguides and leads people into curses and evil, but Jesus restored the power to lead, dominate and influence people for the Kingdom of God. He replaced "serpent leadership" with "servant leadership". A servant leader will fulfil the six purposes that God had set before mankind, being blessed and being a blessing, fruitfulness, multiplication, replenishment, subduing and leading. Like Moses, he will use the staff of leadership to release larger serpents to swallow the smaller serpents of the enemy of our souls. His influence and legacy will outshine and outlive the influence of the serpent leader.

23. THE SOVEREIGNTY OF GOD

"HE HATH EXTENDED MERCY UNTO ME BEFORE THE KING AND HIS COUNSELLORS AND BEFORE ALL THE KING'S MIGHTY PRINCES AND I WAS STRENGTHENED AS THE HAND OF THE LORD MY GOD WAS UPON ME AND I GATHERED TOGETHER OUT OF ISRAEL CHIEF MEN TO GO UP WITH ME."

– **Ezra 7:28**

*W*hen the hand of the Lord our God is upon us, we are greatly strengthened. He will enable us to be viewed favourably by those who are the leaders of the land, their advisers as well as before all other authorities. Ezra and Nehemiah were both given the support and permission of the king of Persia to revive the temple of God and to rebuild the walls of Jerusalem as the Lord extended His mercy towards them. They were able to mobilise men and resources to complete their mission of rebuilding the walls of Jerusalem and the temple of Jehovah. Similarly, we are enabled to take up projects that are ordained by the Lord by giving us favour with the concerned authorities. He will cause our leadership to be effective, purposive and productive.

23. The Sovereignty of God

King Artaxerxes under whom Ezra and Nehemiah served recognised the power, grace and sovereignty of God. He ordered that all the vessels of gold and silver as well as bullion and other provisions required to rebuild the temple be given liberally. He called Ezra the "scribe of the God of heaven." He gave him authority to appoint judges and magistrates and to teach the law of God to the people. Truly, when God gives a man a vision and the anointing to lead, He will change unfavourable circumstances to favourable ones and will give the provision to fulfil the vision. The walls of Jerusalem are a metaphor for our defences. The gates are a symbol of God-given opportunities. The Lord will enable us to rebuild our defences and regain our opportunities. When we seek the Lord with all our heart, His hand of mercy will be upon us. He is waiting to strengthen those whose hearts are set on seeking the Lord and doing His will on earth. Both Ezra and Nehemiah were but bondmen or foreign captives in the Persian Empire. God again proved that spiritual power and influence supercedes the political. Godly leaders exercise such spiritual power and influence in the conduct of their affairs and the fulfilment of their vision.

24. THE LITTLE GREEN LIGHT IN OUR SOULS

"THINE EARS SHALL HEAR A WORD BEHIND THEE, SAYING, 'THIS IS THE WAY, WALK YE IN IT, WHEN YE TURN TO THE RIGHT HAND AND WHEN YE TURN TO THE LEFT.'"

– Isaiah 30:21

When we make decisions, big or small, critical as well as less consequential, it would be good to consult the Lord. When we spend a few moments in prayer, humbling ourselves before God, seeking His wisdom, counsel and guidance, He will speak in a whisper. We will hear a word as if spoken behind our ears along with the flutter or rush of the breeze as if of a dove's wings, saying, "This is the way, walk in it. Do not turn to the right or to the left." As we seek His guidance in prayer, we should wait till we sense an awesome, inexplicable peace, assurance, strength and hope. That is God's little green light by which He guides us into the right decisions and steps of execution. We should also be sensitive to noticing the yellow light or the warning sign and the red light or the stop sign that should stop us in our tracks and keep us from making a move in that direction.

24. The Little Green Light in Our Souls

We should not wait till God opens a donkey's mouth to speak to us and warn us. Both our eyes and our ears and our minds and hearts need to be sensitive to the signals and signs from God. The Holy Spirit is a practising counsellor for us here on earth. He gives us unction or anointing and leading or guidance in all our leadership and management functions in all domains. The word "POSDCORB" sums up all management or leadership functions, planning, organising, staffing, directing, coordinating, reporting and budgeting. The Lord will guide, bless and lead us with a word of wisdom in all these responsibilities that we are called as leaders and managers to perform daily.

He will help us set our goals in a realistic as well as challenging way so that it is feasible as well as beyond our normal reach. When we achieve it, we will realise that without the help and enablement of God, it would have been impossible to accomplish it. The Lord will continually water us right through the day and right through our lives with wisdom and guidance. He will lead us to the right people to recruit or team up with. We will not see the little green light in our souls if there is a lot of chatter in our minds. We need to still our hearts and minds to hear the small and feeble whisper in which the Lord speaks to us. If we are in a great and tearing or unholy haste, we might miss out on seeing the sign or hearing the voice.

We need to learn to wait on the Lord before making the move or taking the plunge. Once the decision is made, we should not swerve to the right or the left in terms of the overall direction though we can be flexible with regard to the strategies we adopt and allow for mid-course learning and corrections. Things sometimes go wrong or we run into some unexpected roadblocks even on the highway God leads us on but He promises that we will never be overpowered by the roaring lion or the beast on this highway. A road other than the one indicated by God's signposts can lead us right into the lion's den. We need to connect every little dot of the actions we take with the big picture of the vision God gives us. What leaders envision, managers implement. When I got the vision of starting Friends of Police, the Lord gave me a green signal on the way I should take step by step. He told me once through prophetic guidance, "You need to form teams of like-minded people to implement your idea."

25. LEADERSHIP EXCELLENCE

"A BISHOP THEN MUST BE BLAMELESS, THE HUSBAND OF ONE WIFE, VIGILANT, SOBER, OF GOOD BEHAVIOUR, GIVEN TO HOSPITALITY, APT TO TEACH."

– I Timothy 3:2

*T*he scripture exhorts believers to aim and strive for leadership excellence. A bishop is a shepherd of shepherds, a leader of leaders. He is one who not only feeds the sheep but feeds the shepherds. Such a person will have his or her name written in the Book of the Shepherd in addition to the Book of the Living. He is like Peter, one who shows his love for God and Christ by feeding the sheep. He is to be blameless in his conduct, in his habits and his private life. He should demonstrate his leadership both at home and in public life by being impeccable and flawless. At the same time, he should not become overconfident, self-righteous or proud. He needs to be watchful not just of the flock he leads but also of himself lest he falls into temptation when his guard is down. He needs to be sober and ever watchful in prayer, believing and exercising the power of prophylactic prayer to pre-empt the enemy of our souls.

A leader must be charitable, generous and hospitable, willing to share what God has blessed him with. Abraham was a great example of generosity and hospitality. He gave his best for the enjoyment of guests who were strangers to him. He was concerned for not just his kith and kin like Lot but all the inhabitants of the land he dwelt in. He should not withhold any good that he can do for anyone. He should not enjoy or encourage either gossip, malice or flattery. With sincerity of conscience, he should hold on to the mystery of godliness. He should not be inconsistent, double-tongued or given to anger, bitterness or strife. He should not be greedy or eager to feather his own nest by exploiting those he leads.

Abraham refused to share the spoils of the king of Sodom. He should be careful to keep his marital vows and stay guarded in his relationship with other women. One of the safeguards that could be useful to prevent one from falling into adultery is to never stay alone in a room with a woman other than one's wife. A leader should be as willing to learn as well as to teach. He should realise that he is not the repository of all knowledge and wisdom about God or the world and humble himself to learn from others. He should realise that he being human and fallible is prone to errors of judgment, unwitting mistakes as well as wanton blunders. He should be willing and hold himself accountable to God and an inner team of counsellors or advisors to be corrected when he goes wrong. He should be diligent in his leadership, not trying to hog the limelight but trying hard to discover and develop the gifts of others so that the whole body grows in Christ and it does not become imbalanced or lop-sided. A credible life is needed to back the incredible claims of Jesus in order to convict people.

26. WEANED LEADERSHIP

"SURELY I HAVE BEHAVED AND QUIETED MYSELF,
AS A CHILD THAT IS WEANED OF HIS MOTHER,
MY SOUL IS EVEN AS A WEANED CHILD."

– Psalms 131:2

Conquerors in history are never contented with their conquest. They want to conquer and annex more land and people. Capitalists are not contented with their great wealth, they always want to multiply it further. Rulers want to add to their power and stature. People want to add to their wealth and resources. Children want more toys. Women want more clothes and shoes. Builders want to build more. Winners want to win more and so on. The list of human wants is endless. We are like children who are never satisfied with the milk we have drunk. We want more and more. Those who want more and more are like immature feeding children, but God's call to us is to be like a child who is weaned, who no longer delights in the things of the world but delights in resting and trusting in God's presence as a weaned child rests calm, assured, contented and secure in her mother's arms.

We are no longer to be concerned with great ambitions for ourselves but we wait calmly and patiently for the Lord to show us what we should do. A weaned child is not a weak child. Our inner strength that is nourished by the grace of the Lord keeps us quiet and secure in the knowledge that the Lord will provide for us, that He will protect us and that He will promote us. We are responsible to consciously still and quieten our hitherto restless souls. Our food and meat that strengthens us are the Word that the Lord provides us day after day. A weaned child is a maturing person. Our physical habits and emotions are predictable even as our thoughts and ideas are unpredictable. A weaned child is a growing child. We do not stop growing all our lives even when we are old. Our growth is intentional and we pursue the goals the Lord sets for us. A weaned child is a well-behaved and considerate person. We are gentle and compassionate, not always concerned only about our own needs and interests but looking to the needs and interests of others.

Leaders are to be weaned from the influences of the world and be influenced by the Word, to be secure but not complacent, to be strong and effective and to be calm but not silent in the face of untruth and injustice. This uni-verse is written by David as the king of Israel. Despite his great power and prowess, he knew that compared with the Lord he was at best only a weaned child. Our contentment, our security, our joy and our peace are found only in the presence of the Lord, a personal relationship with God. We have tasted the Lord's goodness. We are not guilty about our past, anxious about the present or fearful about the future. We are becoming like children ever ready to return to the embrace of our loving Father in heaven. We manifest not a careless attitude but a carefree attitude. We manifest a studied and practised quietness, calmness, assurance, confidence, gentleness, humility and security in all our situations, circumstances and relationships.

27. ROOT, SHOOT, BRANCHES, FRUIT OF LEADERSHIP

"HE SHALL CAUSE THEM THAT COME OF JACOB TO TAKE ROOT. ISRAEL SHALL BLOSSOM AND BUD AND FILL THE FACE OF THE WORLD WITH FRUIT."

– Isaiah 27:6

The Old Testament is the root, the New Testament is the shoot and our lives are the branches with blossom, bud and fruit. He has caused us to rise from the faith of Jacob or Israel and his covenant of faith with Jehovah. The Lord is the author, source and cause of our faith even as He is the creator of our lives. Perhaps, our seeking the light or truth with all our hearts helped in His choosing us. We have been grafted by our personal commitment and faith onto the shoot of Jesse, the father of David, King of Israel and onto his descendant, seed and root Jesus. Jesus is described in the scripture as the Root and offspring of David. If the branches are not strong in faith, they will wither and be cast into the fire to burn. If the branches are not yielding fruit too, they would be cut. If the branches are not growing well enough, it is pruned and trimmed to facilitate healthy growth. Our roots should be strong, our shoot should be evergreen and then the branches will be full of blossom, bud and fruit.

The root, shoot, branches and fruit analysis helps us always have a connected picture of God, the Word and our life and its purpose. We are a planting of the Lord to reveal the splendour of His power, glory and grace. The enemy of our soul would like to lay his axe on our roots. We are marked people as we are responsible for the salvation of many. Therefore, as part of our covenant with God, we need to always have in mind some "root" verses and some "shoot" verses of protection that we erect as an enclosure or fencing around our lives. The enemy is described as a "roaring lion waiting to devour His people." The root promises of protection like Psalm 91 verses 14 and 16 and the shoot verses of blessing are Romans 8 verse 28 and John 14 verse 23.

Even in the natural world, the shoot looks different from the root. The root looks dry, glamourless or sans beauty, shapeless, twisted and dull while the shoot looks green, erect and strong. The shoot verse Romans 8 verse 28 seems quite different from the root verse Psalm 91 verse 14 but they are intimately connected as root to shoot and the root holds the shoot up. With our believing, meditating and praying over and over again through the root and shoot verses, our lives get intimately connected to the shoot and thereby, to the root and we are primed to bear abundant supernatural, spiritual and natural fruit for the glory of God, our planter, gardener and keeper.

The blossoms are what makes us attractive to others just as colourful, scented flowers attract butterflies, bees

27. Root, Shoot, Branches, Fruit of Leadership

and other insects to visit and both receive the nectar of our fellowship and carry forward the pollen of our fruitfulness. Our innumerable natural actions, thoughts and words are the leaves. The buds are our ideas and plans that the Lord enables us to carry to fruition if they are in accordance with His Word and will. The fruit are the words, qualities and actions that satisfy the spiritual hunger of people. The Lord desires that we expand our influence across the whole face of the planet to turn a desert of violence, meaninglessness and accompanying ugliness into a garden of great usefulness, meaning, beauty and fragrance.

28. LION-LIKE LEADERSHIP

"THE REMNANT OF JACOB SHALL BE AMONG THE GENTILES IN THE MIDST OF MANY PEOPLE AS A LION AMONG THE BEASTS OF THE FOREST, AS A YOUNG LION AMONG THE FLOCKS OF SHEEP, WHO, IF HE GOES THROUGH, BOTH TREADETH DOWN AND TEARETH IN PIECES AND NONE CAN DELIVER."

– Micah 5:8

*T*he faithful in every age and nation will remain only a remnant and not the majority. With God on one's side, even one person is more than the majority. He is like a lion, a king or leader among all people. The Lord increases in might the power of the meek. He enables them to defeat the plans and designs of the enemy of their souls, the roaring lion. By their prayers and the judicious exercise of their faith and spiritual power, tread down on strongholds, tear these in pieces and bring down every speculation that rises against the truth and will of God. The use of the opposite metaphors of "lion" and "sheep" in the same breath is to point out that godly leaders though they are lions with immense power should be meek, humble, gentle and obedient like sheep. Jesus though He is portrayed as the "Lion of Judah" was also the "Lamb of God."

28. Lion-Like Leadership

He was led to the slaughter like a lamb though He could have physically destroyed the entire Roman army with His breath. We, too, are called to be like a young lion in terms of courage but gentle like a sheep. Our attitude should be confident like that of a king but our behaviour like that of a servant. This is the essence of the concept of servant-leadership. Our knowledge of God and His Word and ways should not get us all impatient, puffed up and vain but it should teach us to be meek and patient to wait upon His will to be fulfilled in His time. It is said that a pack of lions led by a sheep is far less powerful than a flock of sheep led by a lion.

This underlines the importance the Lord gives to leadership in executing His will. He raised up a man from the papyrus reeds, Moses whose very name meant "reeds" but his deeds and words written on paper today have taught and demonstrated with power to many faithful people every lesson of leadership one needs to learn. The words of Moses put fear in the hearts of the mighty Pharaoh and the Egyptians. His words and his ordinary staff were his weapons. It made his formidable enemies and opponents tremble with fear even as other beasts would before a lion. The reference to "young lion" in the uni-verse is a promise of the Lord to restore and renew our youthful vigour. The scripture refers to it as the "dew of our youth". He will make us fruitful even into our old age. It is the blessing and anointing of the Lord that makes us a "lion" or powerful leader. He invests His authority in us. He makes us his signet ring to authenticate or give the final seal of approval. We have the sword of the Word in one hand and the sword of execution in the other.

29. ACTIVE LEADERSHIP OF THE LORD

"I WILL INSTRUCT THEE AND TEACH THEE IN THE WAY WHICH THOU SHALT GO, I WILL GUIDE THEE WITH MINE EYE."

– Psalms 32:8

*V*ery often in life we take this promise of the Lord for granted and approach Him only when we have messed up on our own, relying on our own native intelligence and knowledge. In matters of knowledge, experiments are more apt. In matters of faith and human life, experience is far more significant. So much is given to the domain of human knowledge and understanding and the rest is all the domain of faith and revelation. A good part of our lives rests in the latter domain. This is the Kingdom of God. It intersects every day with our lives. We should actively seek instruction at the feet of the Lord. We should learn for He promises to teach us the way we should go every day of our lives. He will guide us with His caring eye upon us. As we err and fall, His eye will tell us to pick ourselves up and walk again.

Only God knows the totality of our past, our present and our future. He factors all of that into every direction He gives us. He knows our strengths, weaknesses and desires.

29. Active Leadership of the Lord

He knows our opportunities and threats. We should follow only God as our one true and trustworthy leader. He is the visionary who gives sight to the blind following Him. Even the ablest and best of human leaders are blind. They do not know the shape of the future. As Peter Drucker said, "The only thing we know about the future that we know is that it will be different." By definition, God is the only true leader of humanity. A leader gives directional instruction while a manager gives instructional directions. A leader tells us and shows us the direction in which we should go while a manager gives us the instructions we should follow while on the way.

The Lord is real, active and practical. He wants to engage with our lives in active, practical and real ways. He instructs us from His Word. We need to listen to His Word and meditate on it to understand and apply it to our lives in every possible way. We need to value it more than silver or gold. We need to store it in our hearts like treasure. We need to make it our roadmap and the compass of our lives. The eye the Lord keeps on us is the eye of protection, guidance, care and love. We need to be spiritually sensitive to pick up the signals from His eye movements.

30. THE LEADERSHIP LADDER

"BESIDES THIS, GIVING ALL DILIGENCE, ADD TO YOUR FAITH VIRTUE AND TO VIRTUE KNOWLEDGE."

– 2 Peter 1:5

*T*he leadership ladder that we are called to climb is not a pyramid of positions and titles but it is the ladder of leadership qualities. In the world's paradigm of leadership, the law that applies is that the higher the climb, the greater the fall, but as we climb the ladder of leadership qualities, God will send His angels to assist us and keep us from falling. He also has a safety net called confession to Him and cleansing by His blood, to catch us if and when we fall. A leader's qualities are not cast in stone but are developed over a lifetime. They come from the study of the Word and the constant persistent application of it to our lives. The Word is our yardstick and measuring rod. We should measure our qualities against it and ask the Lord for grace to fulfil His divine standards.

Once we take the first step of faith it should be followed by diligent study of the Word in order to lead up to the next step which is virtue or character. The promises of God are given to us primarily not for meeting our physical needs but to enable us to "partake in the divine nature", to develop the character of Jesus, to learn to be humble

30. The Leadership Ladder

and gentle like Him and to be virtuous. The next step is to increase in knowledge of the love of God, to know the unending dimensions of His agape love, its immeasurable length, breadth, height and depth. The next rung on to which we should climb on Jacob's blessed ladder is self-control. We should hold our desires under control. We should hold our temper under control. We should hold our emotions under control. We should hold our tongue or speech under control. These are signs of maturity and increasing grace and perfection.

The fifth step on the ladder of leadership is patience, the ability to wait with expectation, joy and gratitude for the Lord's will to be done. A desire fulfilled is sweet to the soul but it becomes sweeter the longer we can wait to receive it. The sixth step is godliness or God-like righteousness and integrity. The seventh step is kindness to one's fellow beings, whether above us or below us in the social pecking order. The eighth step is the final step, the highest in God's hierarchy of values, love. Our attainment of these qualities is not achieved overnight but it is a steady progression. We don't climb the ladder of leadership by pushing others down or by holding on to the feet of those above us. We help others also up the ladder as we climb. The leader himself often becomes a ladder for others to climb. Though the ladder looks narrow, there is room for everyone willing to lead and climb. The Lord never wants us to rest on any rung of the ladder but wants us to keep climbing to the next level.

31. OUR GOD CONCEPT

"HEZEKIAH RECEIVED THE LETTER FROM THE HAND OF THE MESSENGERS AND READ IT AND HEZEKIAH WENT UP UNTO THE HOUSE OF THE LORD AND SPREAD IT BEFORE THE LORD."

– Isaiah 37:14

*H*ezekiah, the king of Israel was facing the overwhelming odds of a military confrontation with the formidable army of Sennacherib, king of Assyria. The latter sent a messenger who asked him not to be deceived into believing that the God of Israel could save them from being routed and captured. The letter spoke about the numerous kingdoms that the Assyrian army had already overrun. Hezekiah responded by going to the temple of the Lord and spreading out the letter of Sennacherib before the Lord. Hezekiah first affirmed his faith in God and praised His glorious name. He then sought the help of the Lord remembering how the Lord had helped Israel in the past against mighty enemies and given them great deliverance. The Lord responded by assuring him that their enemies would go back the way they had come.

The same night that the Assyrian army encamped around Jerusalem in readiness to capture it, the Lord sent an angel of death and slew 1,85,000 troops. Sennacherib returned to Nineveh and there he was assassinated by two

31. Our God Concept

of his own sons. In this day and time, each of us face overwhelming odds at times. Instead of being overcome with fear, grief and panic, we should spread our sheet before the Lord and seek the help of His mighty angels. He is Ebenezer God and is always willing to come to the help of the faithful who depend not on their own prowess or ability but the strength of their God. Our faith is dependent on our "God concept" or our understanding of who God is and the extent of His love, mercy and grace towards us. Hezekiah based on his study and knowledge of the history of Israel from the times of Moses had an excellent, "God concept".

Whatever the challenge or difficulty we are facing, we should believe and affirm that God is greater, infinitely greater than the totality of our problems. Going to the house of the Lord in the New covenant context is to search deep within us, in the tabernacle of our own souls where God dwells for His ever-present help. "Spreading our sheet before the Lord" implies laying claim to the promises of God contained in His Word, lying spread-eagled in His presence, surrendering and casting our burdens at His feet. The name "Sennacherib" implies "sin replaced my brothers". It ironically meant that every earthly king relies on sinful or cursed power.

The mightiest power on earth is limited and circumscribed by the sovereign authority of God. The name "Hezekiah" in contrast means, "God is my strength". Each of us is called to be a king Hezekiah in our own domains. Just as God helped Hezekiah safeguard his capital Jerusalem, He will help us guard our capital, our home, our hearts, our health, our possessions, our faith and our well-being from every attack of the sinful enemy. The Lord allows the Sennacherib's of the world to rise against us so that we will have a wonderful testimony or evidence of the faithfulness and reality of God's present, practical and sufficient help in our lives. The most important leadership concept is the God concept. If we have got this concept right, everything else will fall in place.

32. THE JETHRO PARADIGM OF LEADERSHIP

"MOREOVER THOU SHALT PROVIDE OUT OF ALL THE PEOPLE ABLE MEN, SUCH AS FEAR GOD, MEN OF TRUTH, HATING COVETOUSNESS AND PLACE SUCH OVER THEM, TO BE RULERS OF THOUSANDS AND RULERS OF HUNDREDS, RULERS OF FIFTIES AND RULERS OF TENS."

– **Exodus 18:21**

Leadership, it is said, is a combination of strategy and character. If one has to do without one, it is a strategy and not character. Jethro could be called the real father of management and the concept of godly leadership. Jethro was not a Jew but a Midianite. Yet, he feared God. Leadership and wisdom are not the preserve of any one individual or nation. It can come from strange or unexpected quarters. Jethro observed that his son-in-law Moses was wearing himself and the people down by bearing the entire responsibility of hearing their grievances and trying to resolve them. He advised Moses to select men whom Moses should train and teach in applying the law and God's Word. He asked him to choose able men who fear God as fearing God would keep them humble and wise and not become arrogant. Fearing God implied that they would accept the counsel of God received through Moses.

Fearing God implied that they acknowledged God Himself as their ultimate leader. They should also be men of integrity, just men who loved the truth and lived the truth, men who hated covetousness and therefore, would be contented and not take bribes or falsely favour one against the other. Ability is subordinated to character. Character comes before competence in the leadership paradigm. Jethro does not major in ability. He takes it as a given, a starting point or assumption. He did not give any place to strategy. Leadership to him was a combination of a relationship between God and leader, between leader and followers and of ability and character. In short, Jethro's leadership paradigm was a combination of relationship, ability and character.

Only persons with such leadership qualities ought to be given responsibility and authority over others. Moses was taught the principle of delegation by Jethro. Moses was to be left free to commune with God, hear from Him and convey it to the leaders appointed over thousands, hundreds, the fifties and tens. Only the very difficult or great matters were to be brought to Moses while the layers of leaders below would deal with all other matters according to the gravity or importance of the issue. The Hebrew race was used in Egypt to build pyramids but the pyramid became the metaphor for the spiritual bureaucracy to be set up by Moses and his consultant Jethro. Moses should be given credit for listening to his father-in-law's wise advice. Jesus reversed the hierarchical pyramid and went right to the bottom of the pyramid to become the servant of all. He discipled just twelve apostles and ministered to hundreds and thousands. His teachings and example transformed the lives of the apostles and touched the lives of thousands. The latter then taught thousands and that multiplied into millions and even billions through history.

Instead of a pyramid structure today, we should have a core inner circle of leader's protégées. They in turn would have an outer circle whom they influence and that circle of people would influence a larger circle. We can think and pray globally and influence globally. Each person's span of direct impact cannot extend beyond ten to twelve persons whom one can invest his or her life into, but the core principles of leadership remain the same from the time of Jethro, ability or competence to assume responsibility and to lead, loving and living the Word, fear of God, avoiding covetousness or greed and lust, humility and integrity, receiving wisdom and counsel from the Lord. A period of training, mentoring or discipleship should precede a life of ministry. The person mentoring should be someone who has a direct connection with God, a personal relationship with the Lord Jesus and who is consistent in his or her walk with God. A person should not be pitchforked into leading thousands but go through phases of leading tens, the fifties, hundreds and finally, thousands.

33. LEADERSHIP - A TWO-WAY PROCESS

"THOU, O MAN OF GOD, FLEE THESE THINGS AND FOLLOW AFTER RIGHTEOUSNESS, GODLINESS, FAITH, LOVE, PATIENCE, MEEKNESS."

– I Timothy 6:11

Leadership is a two-way process. It is the result of the tension between opposites, between fleeing from the negative and destructive and running after or obsessing and pursuing a principle-based life. A leader needs to flee from temptations, moral traps and foolish and hurtful lusts. He needs to put some distance between these negatives and self and keep increasing the distance so that they never catch up or overtake him. At the same time, he needs to pursue or follow actively after righteousness, godliness, faith, love, patience and meekness. He needs to put away the former and put on the latter. He needs to "be at" the latter and " beat" or overcome the former. He needs to reinforce the positive qualities or attributes and values and negate, weaken or defeat the negative qualities and attributes. When he does so, he is trying to be perfect and trying to imitate God and Christ. Fleeing from the enemy of our souls is one part or one-half of our responsibility. Following the example of Jesus is the better half.

33. Leadership - A Two-Way Process

When we are doing both, we are truly living fully and following fully. We are living an abundant life, a life overflowing with grace and glory. When we are doing both, we are transformed from being mere followers into leaders. God wants His greatness and goodness to be reflected daily in our lives. It is interesting to see how Paul's epistle to his mentee Timothy, in the first letter in I Timothy chapter 3 verses 1 to 13 talks about godly or servant leaders while in the second letter in II Timothy chapter 3 verses 1 to 13 talks about worldly or serpent leaders. He was exhorting Timothy as in this uni-verse to avoid, defeat and overcome the one and to follow, practice and be the other.

Evil weakens the human will. Our spirits should not be adulterated with that which is impure or evil. We need to die to the negatives and live for the positives. This is the thought process that underlies the scripture. It is the process of renewing our minds or renewing our thoughts and emotions and reinvigorating our wills or the capacity to make decisions and follow through on decisions. Joseph renewed his vision for his life by constantly reviewing the God-given dreams he saw as a youth. This enabled him to flee from the temptation of succumbing to the seduction and adultery of Potiphar's wife. He pursued righteousness while in prison. He pursued godliness, love, patience and meekness. It brought him divine favour and kingly favour in due time. Joseph showed love and patience when he wept and embraced his brothers, the very ones who conspired to sell him into slavery.

Faith is just a just foundation to justify us or align us with the plan and vision of God for our lives. We need to edify, sanctify and glorify it further. To edify means to build, strengthen and cause it to grow, to mature. To sanctify means to purify or cause our lives and character to conform to the image of God. To glorify means to allow God's grace and power to flow freely in our lives so that it pleases God, it glorifies Him. For a beautiful edifice or building to come up in a plot where an old house stands, the old house has to be demolished, the foundations dug up, the debris carried away till the last stone and brick are removed and then, the new structure comes up. First, the foundation is dug deep and laid, the pillars come up, the walls are bricked in and the floors tiled, the building is then painted, furnished and finished. Leadership similarly is a demolition and building process in which humility is the leitmotif or continual thread, patience is the cement, righteousness and godliness are the walls and love is the summit.

34. THE LEGACY OF LEADERSHIP

"FOR I KNOW HIM, THAT HE WILL COMMAND HIS CHILDREN AND HIS HOUSEHOLD AFTER HIM AND THEY SHALL KEEP THE WAY OF THE LORD, TO DO JUSTICE AND JUDGMENT, THAT THE LORD BRING UPON ABRAHAM THAT WHICH HE HATH SPOKEN OF HIM."

– **Genesis 18:19**

God knew Abraham personally. It is the first example of a personal relationship based on commitment and mutual trust. God tested Abraham's faith in a variety of ways. Abraham passed every test. He was greatly blessed and was a channel of blessings to others. Can God speak of each of us with such confidence as He spoke of Abraham? Are we esteemed of God like Abraham and Daniel? Do we trust God with the same magnitude and manner of faith? We too are not to dam up our blessings but circulate them to others so that they too increase in faith and be blessed. God gave Abraham incredible promises. He fulfilled them in impossible conditions. Faith makes it possible to imagine it is possible. Nothing is impossible or too difficult for God. Likewise, as we are made in the image of God and restored after the fall of man again by Jesus with a double portion of blessings, by our faith in Him nothing is impossible or difficult for us. The image of God is not imaginary but real.

It is the character or the essence of who God is. An essence contains the quality, taste and smell of that from which it is extracted, for example, the universally loved vanilla essence for ice creams is extracted from the vanilla plant. Our lives and our character should be tinged with the essence of the quality and character of God. God was disappointed with Israel when they asked for a king like other nations. He knew the leadership of men would be fallible and prone to error as proved by the leadership of Saul and even the one commended as being after God's own heart, David. He wanted Israel to be led by His law. Today, He wants us to follow the leadership of His Word. His Word, not another human being or human teaching, is to lead us all our days on earth. His Word is interpreted and recalled by the power of the Holy Spirit.

We should keep the way of the Lord as revealed in His Word. His ways are just and good. His judgment is wise. Justice, goodness and wisdom should be the hallmark of our lives. We should turn the great teachings of the Lord into principles, the principles into habits and the habits into legacy and then we experience the glory of God and manifest the greatness of God. Like Joshua, we and our children after us are called and committed to serving the Lord. We are to share, exemplify and teach our children to diligently study the Word, to obey the precepts and to allow their inner being to be taught and shaped by the Lord through His Word. We are to talk about it when we rise, when we lie down, when we walk with them, when we dine with them, when things are going good and when it is not so good. By doing so we pass on the baton of faith to the next generation and inspire them to do it with their next.

The uni-verse ends with a promise. Everything in life is a promise to live by. Every currency note is just a promise of the state or government to pay the bearer a certain sum of money. It has value because the one who is making the promise for the state has the wherewithal it is assumed to make good its promise. Likewise, knowing personally and not just formally or impersonally who God is, we are assured that He always makes good His promise, however impossible or difficult it might seem. The Lord will cause to bring upon us as He did with Abraham that which He promised or spoke into and upon our lives and that of our children.

35. TRIPLE ROLE- WITNESS- LEADER- COMMANDER

"BEHOLD, I HAVE GIVEN HIM FOR A WITNESS TO THE PEOPLE, A LEADER AND COMMANDER TO THE PEOPLE."

– Isaiah 55:4

*I*n this world, we have witnessed only negative events, crimes, accidents and misdemeanours but we do not examine witnesses who speak of the positive, the truth, the good events and happenings. A leader is a witness of the truth to the people who follow him. Jesus is given by God as a witness to people of the truth about God, eternal life and salvation. He is the Prince of peace not by virtue of the royal garments or royal residence or titles or wealth or high birth but by virtue of the witness He gave of God Almighty. Jesus is the perfect leader who asked nothing for Himself and gave Himself fully. He is given as a covenant to the people. He stands surety for God's promises.

The greatest men who walked on earth looked for leadership to Jesus, be it the saints of the New Testament times or men like M.K. Gandhi or Martin Luther King Jr. The principles He taught are counterintuitive, to resist evil and overcome evil not with greater evil but by holding on to the truth. Jesus unlike them is not just a historical

35. Triple Role- Witness- Leader- Commander

personality who is no more, but He remains a living witness to our spirits. He leads us and commands us every day of our lives. He is given all power and authority in heaven and on earth. We, too are called to be His witnesses. Daniel wrote that the wise who lead many into righteousness are like the stars that shine forever. When we witness the truth of Jesus, we too become leaders and commanders. As witnesses for Jesus, we speak of what we have seen, heard and experienced. As witnesses, we are only expected to be truthful and we do not have to exaggerate anything. As leaders, we lead many into righteousness.

Knowing Jesus and emulating Him is wisdom. We drink daily at the fount of His wisdom and knowledge, the Word of God. We are set free when we surrender our minds to Jesus and our thoughts to His Word. Our yoke or bondage to this world is broken. We can then lead many into freedom and righteousness. Obeying the commands of God makes us commanders to the people. Jesus has delegated all power and authority that He enjoys in Heaven and on earth to His commanders on earth. We too can command sickness to be healed, spirits to depart and peace to descend.

36. THE GRACE OF LEADERSHIP

"FOR PHYSICAL TRAINING IS OF SOME VALUE, BUT GODLINESS HAS VALUE FOR ALL THINGS, HOLDING PROMISE FOR BOTH THE PRESENT LIFE AND THE LIFE TO COME"

– Timothy 4 : 8

It is the destiny of the followers of Jesus to be influential leaders. The mantle of godly leadership falls on those who listen carefully to the commandments of God, diligently study these and apply them in every area and domain of life. The word "hear" in this context expands to mean "hear, enjoy, apply and rejoice". Most believers are good at supplication but not at application. It is an application that shows the extent of our faithfulness. We do not have to fight to achieve leadership positions but the Lord will orchestrate matters such that the believer and the applier become the head or leader. As we study the Word and apply it in our lives, we receive the anointing or the empowerment to be leaders, the grace of leadership. We will rise above circumstances, however adverse and not sink under them. We will hold our heads up high in hope and confidence and not let them hang in shame or bow in fear.

36. The Grace of Leadership

Leadership is a divine calling and this is the reason why most earthly leaders fall or fail. They have all the charisma and gifting. Yet, they will be embroiled in one scandal or controversy or folly in the things they do or say in the course of their leadership. Take John F. Kennedy, a charismatic leader but the last has not been written of his sexual escapades while in the White House. Princess Diana who won the hearts of the English people as well as admirers worldwide for her philanthropy and for espousing good causes had a series of clandestine affairs in reaction to her husband Prince Charles' infidelity. Even business or corporate leaders plunge in terms of esteem due to some peccadillo or other. In the Old Testament times, a great Babylonian emperor like Nebuchadnezzar had to be humbled due to his exalting himself to the level of being a god. David, a man after God's own heart, in a moment of weakness fell to the temptation of adultery and what amounted to murder in the eyes of God. Godly leaders are assertive, not aggressive. They will not let the tail wag the dog of leadership. They are firm but humble. They take principled stands on issues and are prepared to pay the price for it.

The Lord will not only make us the head but He will give us a head of wisdom and a heart of compassion. We will develop and use the qualities of head and heart that are needed for effective leadership. One has to subject oneself constantly to the leadership of God, the Holy Spirit. He will give us the calling or the field in which we should work, the gifting or abilities needed for such a calling and the qualities that should adorn such a calling. The so-called secular or worldly paradigm of leadership has only these three components, knowledge, skills and attitudes, but, God-ordained leadership consists of Beliefs, Attitudes, Skills, Knowledge or BASK. Belief is the good root that gives rise to the good shoot and the good fruit. The belief in God and trust in His character are fundamental to leadership. The perspective of earthly leaders ends with a lifetime while the perspective of godly leaders arcs over into eternity. The concern or focus of earthly leaders could be the physical, economic or social well-being of the followers while the focus of godly leaders is holistic. Godly leaders tap into the supernatural power of their God, Creator and Redeemer by making a pact with God such that He is their best friend, constant companion, wonderful counsellor, shrewd business partner and faithful life partner. Worldly leaders check if they have the resources while godly leaders check if God is present with them.

37. LEADERS AS SPIRITUAL WATCHMEN FOR THE NATIONS

"I WILL STAND UPON MY WATCH AND SET ME UPON THE TOWER AND WILL WATCH TO SEE WHAT HE WILL SAY UNTO ME AND WHAT I SHALL ANSWER WHEN I AM REPROVED."

– **Habakkuk 2:1**

The uni-verse de-romanticises the role of leadership. No great titles or high-sounding epithets. We are just watchmen. The Lord has appointed us as watchmen for our respective nations and organisations. A leader is a watchman for the Lord. He watches happenings in this world and reports them faithfully to the Lord and He takes the message from the Lord and communicates it to the world. We are to watch it all day and all night. We are expected to be vigilant and alert. We are to take a stand on virtually every aspect of life and be a witness in every area or domain of life. We are to examine and analyse the trends and reach a conclusion of what is the Lord's will. We are to watch out for the souls of the people we are leading as a shepherd is concerned for his sheep. We are to be sensitive to what the Lord is speaking into our lives and be attentive to His Word.

We are the Chief Spiritual Officers of our organisations and nations. Each of us has a specific jurisdiction or area to watch over. The Lord gives us the tools of the watchman, the flashlight of the Holy Spirit to search the scripture and discover life-saving and life-enhancing truths, the cane or stick of authority, the whistle to raise the alarm and call the angels to our help, a notebook in which to record our observations, thoughts and feelings. Our lives are divided into different watch hours of the night. Our hope and joy increase as the dawn draws near and we are about to be called to make our final report before the Lord.

As spiritual watchmen, we are responsible for the inner security and sense of well-being of people. We must watch out for the attacks of the roaring lion and warn people of these risks and dangers. As watchmen, we are not to leave our posts or abdicate our responsibilities. We should be faithful and diligent. We ward off attacks by mounting the prayer tower and spending time in prayer. Prayer gives us a strategic height to have a commanding view of what lies ahead of us, the nation and the world. Jesus described satan as a thief, robber and killer. As watchmen, our role is to reduce the extent of his thieving, robbery and killing. We can through our active prayer life and intercession focus on pre-empting him from stealing and robbing lives, peace, health and eternity from people.

We can prevent satan from killing the faith and souls of people. A watchman should have a keen sense of vision. What he sees and hears, he needs to accurately and promptly report to the Lord. It is the Lord who acts on our

37. Leaders as Spiritual Watchmen for the Nations

prayer reports. Spiritual watchmen unlike the watchmen of the world report the positive and the praiseworthy. They send up prayer reports as well as praise reports. At times when the Lord is about to reproach or rebuke or punish, the watchman stands in the gap and intercedes for people. Abraham was a watchman for the world during his lifetime. He pleaded for the lives of people living nearby. Moses was a watchman for Israel.

38. BLIND VERSUS VISIONARY LEADERSHIP

"LET THEM ALONE, THEY ARE BLIND LEADERS OF THE BLIND AND IF THE BLIND LEAD THE BLIND, BOTH SHALL FALL INTO THE DITCH."

– Matthew 15:14

We may not be visually impaired but suffer from blindness of the spirit. Spiritually blind people cannot lead people as they will not have a sense of direction or a sense of right and wrong. They will not be able to know what paths to take, what hurdles to avoid or overcome and what lies ahead of them. The spiritually blind people will blindly follow such leaders to their own fall and destruction. We have many instances of such leadership across the globe and throughout history. One glaring example is that of Hitler who was blinded by hatred and a mistaken sense of his own destiny and that of his race led Germany and a whole lot of people in several nations into destruction. Thankfully, ever since Germany was defeated and the people saw the sheer folly of their ways, she has had sober leadership.

The extremist religious forces of the Middle East are following such a policy of extermination and eventual self-destruction. Only Jesus as Commander-in-Chief of

38. Blind versus Visionary Leadership

the armies of heaven and saints or saved sinners of the earth led by example and from the frontline. He went ahead of us and embraced death, a cruel painful death. All other commanders or leaders embraced safety by either remaining behind their troops like Napoleon or Hitler in his bunker. They would give the excuse that they need to remain safe to provide leadership. Blind leaders might also espouse high ideals of sacrifice, love and service but it would be as a camouflage, disguise or figleaf to delude their blind followers and to cover the nakedness of their pursuit of power for power's sake.

We see in the races for the presidency in the USA and elsewhere when candidates suddenly claim to be Bible believers for long. Blind leaders have an excuse for every misleading action while visionary leaders have a conviction driving them to take risks, to place themselves in the line of fire. Jesus in the first words in this universe, "Let them alone" asks us to ignore or reject blind leadership. Visionary leaders convert the teachings of Jesus into values, the values into principles, the principles into actions and habits and the habits into influence and legacy. The values are the guideposts that light up their paths on this earth. The principles are the paths they take. They have set their eyes like flint on their destination, divine and eternal. Yet, they do all they can to leave the people they lead better in every way and this is their legacy of blessedness. Each of us has blind spots that make us "strain a gnat and swallow a camel" as Jesus put it. We ignore the huge beams that blind our vision of life and take pride in pointing out the specks in our neighbour's or colleagues' eyes. The Word of God holds an accurate mirror to us that enables us to see our hidden blind spots.

The followers of a person pay a great price for the faults and failures of their leader. It is therefore very important that the light of God's Word is focused on the dark areas of leadership, our weaknesses of pride, desire and ambition. When the light of the Word is focused long enough and we heed it, giving priority to His leading over our own feelings and thoughts, the dark areas of leadership will be lit up. Only the Lord is qualified to lead us by example and precept. He knows where we are, what our strengths and weaknesses are and where we should go. He knows the exact direction in which we should move and the pace at which we should move. Instead of leaning on our own or others' blighted intellect and limited vision, we should daily seek the direction the Lord wants us to take in our lives.

We should seek His guidance at every step and turn. We need His help and enablement as many of the things affecting our lives are not visible to the naked eye but have deep and invisible spiritual dimensions. We need His help to prevent and pre-empt us from pressing our own self-destruction buttons. We need His help to prevent us from being deluded or deceived into following others who knowingly or otherwise are leading us up a slippery garden path to a pit of folly, destruction or loss. The implication is that only godly leadership that is dependent on God's grace and wisdom is dependable. Such leadership seeks His kingdom and His righteousness or gives topmost priority to doing God's will on earth. Such leadership will not

38. Blind versus Visionary Leadership

take people on the path of red herrings but on the straight and narrow path that leads upward into eternity. Such leadership is visionary leadership. Such leaders display a singleness of mind and are not easily side-tracked or distracted. Their heads are on their shoulders and their hearts are in the right place. They are conscious and mindful of their great responsibility to lead and not to mislead or misguide those who follow them sincerely and faithfully.

39. THE PRIEST-KING TYPE OF LEADERSHIP

"EZRA THE PRIEST BROUGHT THE LAW BEFORE THE CONGREGATION BOTH OF MEN AND WOMEN AND ALL THAT COULD HEAR WITH UNDERSTANDING, UPON THE FIRST DAY OF THE SEVENTH MONTH."

– **Nehemiah 8:2**

*E*zra was the priest who taught what God wants and Nehemiah was the executive leader, a representative of the king who could get things done. While Ezra's focus was building the faith and knowledge of God in people, the focus of Nehemiah was the physical rebuilding of the walls and ruins of Jerusalem. Today, the offices of priests and the executive or king are combined in each believer. Each of us is meant to be a blend of priestly grace and humility as well as executive firmness and power. Ezra taught the law to the people. They heard him with understanding, implying they heard to obey, to comply with God's commands and to apply. Like Ezra, we have internal work and like Nehemiah, external work. Ezra had an inward vision while Nehemiah had an outward vision. We are called and challenged to be mighty and gracious in word and deed.

39. The Priest-King Type of Leadership

Ezra was the symbol of the fear of God, holiness, reverence and wisdom. Each of us is expected to hear the Word with an understanding as the first thing every day of our lives and to apply it in all areas of our lives. Only when we become doers of the Word do we show that we have truly understood and respected the Word. Or else we would be like the son in one of Jesus's parables who heard his father's instructions and went ahead and did none of it. The people heard the Word read by Ezra with attentiveness. It moved them to tears as they were convicted of falling short of the standards of God. People of this world believe in good times and bad times, good signs and bad omens, but for the believer, every day is precious, every month is significant and every moment is valuable. We need to pay attention to the promptings of the Holy Spirit every moment of our lives.

We need to be reminded of the Word, of both the commands and the promises of God. As priest-kings of Jesus on earth, we are to read the Word and make it understood by the people we are influencing for the Kingdom of God. The purpose of the uni-verse concept is an Ezra-like ministry that touches all parts of the globe. We are given a double anointing, first, as priests and second, as kings. As priests, we are expected to be gentle, compassionate and humble like Jesus. This is the velvet glove that should appear to all. As kings, we are expected to have an iron hand of firmness, determination and authority. It is our divine calling to be a priest-king. This identity colours and is overlaid over our earthly vocation or professions. If one is a doctor, his or her Triune calling is priest-king-doctor. If one is a police officer, he is a priest-king-police officer. If one is an HR manager, his Triune calling is a priest-king-HR manager. If one is a housewife, she is a priest-king-housewife. This is how the promise of God of leadership or headship for the faithful and obedient is fulfilled, "I will make you the head and not the tail. I will make you above and not below." We are not the tail, nobody can wag us or shake us or cause us to act to their whims and fancies like a puppet. We are the head and we should use it to think clearly, think ahead and think like Jesus.

40. GOD'S LEADERSHIP AND GODLY LEADERSHIP

> "SO HE FED THEM ACCORDING TO THE INTEGRITY OF HIS HEART AND GUIDED THEM BY THE SKILLFULNESS OF HIS HANDS."
>
> – **Psalms 78:72**

*T*he only person capable of providing perfect leadership is God. This is the reason it is said that without God our life is like a pointless pencil. Any life and leadership without God is a spiritually blind life and leadership. He enables us to be sharpened and useful. Only the Lord is truthful, completely honest and faithful. The integrity of His heart is absolute. Hence, we can rely upon Him. He is the good shepherd who feeds His sheep. He knows the terrain and the territory through which He leads and guides us. He leads us by still waters where we will find refreshing. He leads us to green pastures where we can feed. He defends us against the wild beast and predators. He leads, guides and protects us with skillfulness.

Leadership without factoring in God and His Word is like surgery without a surgeon. It can be disastrous, dangerous, risky, costly, foolish and has a remote chance of success or efficacy. This uni-verse shows that leadership consists of beliefs, attitudes, skills and knowledge. Beliefs cannot be proved but can be experienced. Once we have tasted the goodness of the Lord and His instructions, we will not depart from these. Our attitudes are evidenced in our conduct, words and actions flow from our core beliefs. Our skills develop as we use our abilities, gifts and talents and practice these over a long period. The natural skills the Lord implants in us at birth, the skills we learn and develop during our lives and the gifts of anointing that we receive as supernatural gifts at the time of our being born again are to be honed and used to the fullest potential and for His glory.

Our knowledge involves an element of paying attention to certain facts, remembering these facts, understanding their implications and applying it to our lives. God's knowledge of us is complete and total. Hence, even to know ourselves the best way is to know God better. He focuses His light on the dark areas of our lives, our hearts and our leadership. Leaders who do not have faith in God and hence, do not have a personal relationship with Him are not able to be victorious in their dark areas. Their greatest defeat and humiliation arise in these dark areas. This aspect underlines the importance of godly leadership in this world. Thinking and writing about life and leadership necessarily centres around godly leadership.

To maintain the integrity of our hearts, we should make ourselves fully accountable to the Lord. We need to invite the Lord to examine our hearts constantly and show us where we have gone wrong or are going wrong. We should measure ourselves against the yardstick of God's Word and not use man's relative standards of comparison.

40. God's Leadership and Godly Leadership

When we voluntarily submit our hearts to the Lord, He will set right our attitudes and help us align them with our beliefs, values and principles. David, the shepherd, tuned his heart like a harp to resonate with the heart of the Lord as evidenced in the Psalms he wrote and sang, but David, the successful king, began to rest on his oars and reduced his dependence on the Lord.

He was distracted and strayed into adultery and wanton killing of one of his soldiers, Uriah in order to marry his wife, but the Lord guided him back to righteousness by sending Samuel with a word of reproach and correction. David repented and humbled himself. He was restored to the integrity of heart, fellowship with the Lord and salvation though he had to pay a heavy price even during his lifetime on earth. The Lord recognises that we change with each stage in our lives and He sends different types of guidance and correction our way. Each command of God is a pointer or pathway that leads up to a pasture or promise or blessing, temporal, spiritual and eternal. Under the old covenant leadership, the kingly, priestly and prophetic offices were kept separate but now under the new covenant leadership, the kingly, priestly and prophetic offices are combined. The new life and leadership are holistic, comprehensive, powerful and effective. It is a combination of a blend of power and grace, privilege and purpose, humility and firmness, gentleness and effectiveness.

41. LEADER AS WATCHMAN

WATCH THEREFORE, FOR YOU KNOW NEITHER THE DAY NOR THE HOUR.

– **Matthew 25 V 13**

*L*eadership is a lot like the duties and position of a watchman. A watchman is not the owner of the house but a servant employed and rewarded with wages to do his duties. The Lord is the owner of the house. We are like watchmen anointed not appointed by the Lord. We wait not to warn people of dangers but to hear the Word of the Lord and pass it on to the people. A watchman lives not in terms of hours but in terms of the hours of watch, two to three hours. A spiritual watchman watches not at night but during every hour of the day. A watchman seeks a strategic point to watch. The strategic points or vantage points are the early hours of the day and the small hours of the night when we wait on the Lord in prayer. A watchman uses his eyes to look out for approaching strangers and dangers, but we use our inner ear and vision to look out for signs and directions from the Lord. When we are questioned, the Lord will give us the Word to speak.

The answer to our mouths lie with the Lord. What do we look out for? We need to carry what we see, hear and feel to the Lord in prayer and He will send His message as well as His messengers to the world. A watchman is

41. Leader as Watchman

also like a shepherd who watches his flock. We need to observe the flock or people we are responsible for and do what is required for their well-being. We need to be alert, sensitive and vigilant like watchmen. The Psalmist says that we should be eager to look out for the Lord and His Word more than watchmen wait for the dawn which is a sign that they can rest. The Holy Spirit will lay on our hearts the burdens of the Lord, the things He is concerned about.

Our own burdens and concerns He will lift. The things we stand for in our professions and lives to mark out the issues of concern that we should look out for. The Lord in turn will watch our backs as we take a stand for Him in this world. When we stake our faith in a promise in God's Word, we are setting ourselves up on a tower, a tower being a metaphor for a vantage point, a place of security, defence and sufficient provision, a position of prominence and pre-eminence.

42. LEADERSHIP FROM STRENGTH TO STRENGTH

"NOW THERE WAS A LONG WAR BETWEEN THE HOUSE OF SAUL AND THE HOUSE OF DAVID, BUT DAVID WAXED STRONGER AND STRONGER AND THE HOUSE OF SAUL WAXED WEAKER AND WEAKER."

– **2 Samuel 3:1**

David had an intimate and personal relationship with the Lord while Saul had distanced himself. Saul departed from the Lord who had chosen and anointed him. Saul was afflicted with the spirit of jealousy against David. Ever since the people hailed David as greater than Saul, he sought to take the life of David, but since the Lord was with David, He preserved his life against all attempts of Saul to have him killed. David had a humble beginning but his end was great. God had chosen and anointed him. He remained faithful to the Lord. The Lord made David stronger and stronger while Saul became weaker and weaker. The weapons and strategies forged by Saul against David just did not seem to prosper. True leadership's trajectory is not like that of a meteor, burning brightly only to burn out. It increases from strength to strength.

42. Leadership from Strength to Strength

A leader who relies on the Lord for grace will go from strength to strength. Each trouble, trial or challenge will not exhaust him but becomes instrumental to moving him to the next level of intimacy with the Lord, of faith, of strength, power and influence, of righteousness and integrity. He will not see a decline in his powers. Setbacks, if any, will be momentary or temporary. He will bounce back with increased vigour and confidence. He will experience struggles but will triumph in the end. Even as he struggles or fights, the Lord will fill him with his joy and power. Doing God's will or what delights the Lord gives him both joy and strength. It is written in the Word that the path of the righteous gets brighter as they go. In contrast, the path of the wicked is filled with darkness and they do not know over what they will stumble.

The path that David travelled on was lit with the precepts and the presence of the Lord. He desired to be just in the eyes of the Lord. Even when he fell, he repented and avoided that error again in his life. God delivered Saul into his hands but David did not choose to lay his hand upon a king who had been once anointed by the Lord. He thereby showed his fear of God. David is not a solitary example of the "anointed of the Lord" leader becoming stronger and stronger. We see it in numerous other examples like that of Mordecai in the time of Esther, the queen. Even Zeresh, the wife of Haman had the insight to recognise that Mordecai being of the seed of Israel would prevail over her once powerful husband Haman. She saw the beginning of the fall of Haman and the rise of Mordecai. Mordecai became stronger and stronger even as Haman grew weaker. Even as our bodies and minds become naturally weaker as we age, our spirits should wax stronger as we lean or depend on the Lord even more than before. Our enemies or foes fight in vain against us for the Almighty Jehovah Nissi fights the war on our behalf. Victory is certain and defeat is not an option.

43. GOD GOVERNANCE AND SELF LEADERSHIP

"HE MAKEST MEN AS THE FISHES OF THE SEA, AS THE CREEPING THINGS, THAT HAVE NO RULER OVER THEM?"

– **Habakkuk 1:14**

Good governance is no substitute for God governance. When Jesus and the Holy Spirit rule over us, we do not need an earthly ruler. We will instinctively like the fish of the sea go in the right direction and be able to successfully negotiate any storm in our lives. Jesus is the model of humanity, divinity and leadership for every one of us. When we think like Jesus, we will also feel, act and live like Him. No more fight or flight but we will flow and overflow with peace, grace and power. Jesus taught us all the leadership lessons we need. He came into the earth from His heavenly home with one purpose, to save mankind. We too should identify one purpose for which we live. In this sense, we should not be like the fish, reptiles, ants and all other creatures, that have only one purpose to survive from day to day. Jesus showed us that while the fittest among us can only survive like the fish, the ants and other creatures, the faithful thrive.

We will not be tempted by the bait of the enemy of our souls. We will not be caught in the snare of his nets. We will open our mouths like fish all the time to praise God and the Lord will fill them. He will fill our mouths with good news to share and great news to break. He will not withhold any good thing from us. Jesus showed us how to be humble and gentle. He taught us to be loving and forgiving. He set an example of serving others. He washed His disciples' feet. He had compassion for the sick and suffering. He wept for His dead friend Lazarus. He is the Wonderful Counsellor, Mighty God, Everlasting King and Prince of Peace. He rules over us not with fear and intimidation but with love and peace. He accomplished His purpose on earth and in heaven.

He revealed the loving nature of the Father. He transplanted the DNA or divine nature into mankind. He taught us the value of faith and how faith can help us surmount the greatest barriers and problems in our lives. He pointed us to the perfection and beauty of the holiness of the Father and asked us to be likewise perfect and holy, to be set apart for God. He taught us to have the unity of a school of fish so that we move in a synchronised and united way. The Holy Spirit is the ruler the Lord Jesus sent to us, to abide with us and in us. He is the counsellor, the comforter, the remembrancer. He reminds us and prompts us. He guides and leads us into all truths. We receive gifts of character and power from the Holy Spirit. He will teach us to be wise and to learn from everything and every word that is spoken to us.

43. God Governance and Self Leadership

    We will learn to work hard in summer and prepare for the winter of our lives like the ants that have no leader, guide or overseer. Most of the time right through history and even today, most human beings cannot lead themselves, let alone others. They end up living a double life, one meant for the eyes of the public and one that is lived in private. Jesus and the Holy Spirit teach us and instruct us in self-leadership. Jesus is the One who holds us together and is integrated as one even as the joints and ligaments hold the body together. He taught us to be anchored in the Holy Spirit. Every day as I feed the fish in our little aquarium, I see them rushing to feed on the tiny pellets of fish food. Similarly, we should rush and feed on the Word the Holy Spirit speaks into our souls. The food that the fish feed on gives them energy while the Word we feed on gives us strength and direction, confidence and hope. So much so, we do not need an earthly leader or rulers like the fish and the ants.

44. SUPERNATURAL LEADERSHIP

"THEN SAID HE UNTO ME, 'FEAR NOT, DANIEL, FOR FROM THE FIRST DAY THAT THOU DIDST SET THINE HEART TO UNDERSTAND AND TO CHASTEN THYSELF BEFORE THY GOD, THY WORDS WERE HEARD AND I HAVE COME FOR THY WORDS.'"

– **Daniel 10:12**

From the first day that Daniel committed his life to the Lord, his prayers were heard by the Lord. He had set his heart to understand and to repent on behalf of his people, Israel before God. The Lord sent his messengers, the angel to Daniel to strengthen him and to give him help to interpret the signs and times. It was revealed to Daniel that a prince of Greece, Alexander the Great would rise to conquer Persia and a large part of the then-known world. These revelations were given to Daniel centuries before Alexander the Great was born. Alexander and the Greek empire represented the kingdom of bronze in the magnificent statue of Nebuchadnezzar's dream. Alexander, Nebuchadnezzar and their like were natural leaders who revelled in physical power but we are called to be supernatural leaders like Daniel, Moses and Jesus.

44. Supernatural Leadership

We become conducting rods for God's miraculous power to flow through us.

Both Alexander and Jesus died at the same age, thirty-three but Alexander's glory and greatness faded with time while Jesus' greatness, territory and glory are expanding. We as watchmen of the Lord need to humble ourselves and set our hearts to understand and discern God's will for our lives in the times we live in. Our humility is not the modesty we put on show before other people but it is the attitude of humility before God. It is knowing that though we are the worst of sinners, God can use us. We make ourselves attractive to the Lord when we are steadfast in seeking His will, Word and wisdom. He will move heaven and earth on our behalf as He did for Daniel. He will hear our petitions and bless us. An answer to our prayers is like a kiss from the Lord on our lips. It is an affirmation that the Lord esteems us as He esteemed Daniel.

Prayer is like a stairway to heaven while praise and worship are an elevator. The Lord will reveal many things to us as He did to Daniel. We will excel in divine knowledge of the extent of the love of the Lord for us, of the extent of His mercy and goodness as well as the awesomeness of His power. God will send His angelic messengers to us. He will touch us and strengthen us. He will speak a word to remove all fear and to encourage us. He will make known the outline of the future. Even while we are praying, He will answer us. Alexander the Great proved the vanity of conquests, the vanity of power, the vanity of fame and greatness, the vanity of wealth and territory. Jesus is the cornerstone that is not cut with human hands-on account of His immaculate birth. He is the cornerstone that makes each of us greater than Alexander for we are more than conquerors. This cornerstone shall fill all nations. Unlike the third horn that stood for Alexander and could be cut off, we will increase in power, grace and influence as we continue to fellowship with the Spirit, dwell on His Word and seek to understand and do His will.

45. FAIL PROOF ROCK SOLID LEADERSHIP

"THE LORD, HE IT IS THAT DOTH GO BEFORE THEE, HE WILL BE WITH THEE, HE WILL NOT FAIL THEE, NEITHER FORSAKE THEE, FEAR NOT, NEITHER BE DISMAYED."

– **Deuteronomy 31:8**

The Lord goes before those who are faithful. His presence is with us. He moves before us as a consuming fire by night to shield us from the powers of darkness and as a cloud to protect us from the troubles of the day. This uni-verse as well as numerous other verses in the scripture reiterate that the Lord will never fail us or forsake us. This one fact is enough to give us an absolute and unshakable sense of security. It will enable us not to fear anything or anyone. It will keep us from disappointment, regret, sadness or discouragement. Moses spoke these words to Joshua as he had experienced the truth of this promise and wanted to pass on the baton of leadership and the anointing to his successor Joshua.

Very often in life, we try to overtake the Lord and try to get ahead, but if we slow down and allow Him to go ahead, He will straighten, smoothen and make safe our paths. We will not suffer unnecessary disappointment, discouragement, fear or sorrow. This implies that before we take any decision, we should pray and seek the Lord's guidance and peace. Even Moses erred in acting impulsively in striking the rock instead of speaking to it to yield water. The Lord is like a rock in terms of His immense and immeasurable strength, His willingness and humility to be the foundation on which we build our lives and His constancy and unchanging nature as against the many changes we undergo. The rock is a metaphor for God our Father, Creator and Redeemer.

It amounts to striking Him or hurting Him when we disregard His wise counsel and seek to do as we please. When we speak to the Rock or pray to Him, He will pour out wisdom like water. The talisman of successful life and leadership is the presence or a continual relationship with the Lord. Our security should not be based on our position, affluence, talents, beauty, glamour or influence but on our relationship with the Rock as Moses went on to describe God the Father who formed us and created us in His image. It is based on the assurance that the Lord will never leave us and that if His presence is with us by day and night, we will never be found wanting in anything. His grace is sufficient to meet all our needs.

This is a present reality as well as a future and eternal hope. We will not be overwhelmed by the heavy odds and formidable enemies and foes we face in life. Adversity will test our faith but it will drive us to dig our heels in and come even closer to the Lord who not only provides for our physical, emotional, familial, social and spiritual needs but also protects and redeems us from our own wilful faults

45. Fail Proof Rock Solid Leadership

and errors. Grace is the cement of love, hope and strength that the Lord pours into the many cracks in our faith wall. We go through ups and downs in our moods, days, fortunes, health, popularity and so on but the Lord looks for consistency in our relationship and our dependence on His unseen presence. The invisibility or "unseenness" of His presence with us is no doubt challenging but the example as well as the errors of Biblical leaders like Moses encourages and builds our faith.

Everything else and everyone else forsakes or fails us as it happened with Job but the Lord will never fail us. He is Himself our shield and exceeding reward as He will certainly exceed our expectations. Success is certain for those who hope in the Lord and walk close with Him for He is able to do far more than we can ask, think or even imagine. We only need to attribute all credit or glory due to Him and not try to steal it or hide it. Immediately after Moses exhorted Joshua with these words, he broke into a kind of swan song, his last song of praise and glory to God wherein He recounted all the great things the Lord had done in and through the nation of Israel. In this whole song, there is not one line in which he himself takes any credit for leading the nation of Israel out of captivity, for the courage with which he challenged the authority of Pharaoh and asked him, "Let my people go." If Abraham was the true father of the nation of Israel and of faith, Moses was virtually the first freedom fighter in history. Yet, he sought only to glorify and adore the Lord.

46. LEADERS ARE CLIMATE CHANGERS

"THE WOMAN SAID TO ELIJAH, NOW BY THIS I KNOW THAT THOU ART A MAN OF GOD AND THAT THE WORD OF THE LORD IN THY MOUTH IS TRUTH."

– I Kings 17:24

*E*lijah was a nobody who came from somewhere in the 9th century BC Israel. His ancestry was not known. He came from Tishbe in Gilead and was called Elijah, the Tishbite. The name "Elijah" means "Jehovah is my God." His name proclaimed his faith in Jehovah. God clothed him with power on high. There are different kinds of power the Lord bestows on His chosen vessels: sustaining power, overcoming power, overwhelming power and wonder-working power. All types of power were manifested in Elijah's life. He had overwhelming power for when he said that it would not rain or drop dew for three years, God confirmed the Word of his mouth as truth.

The Lord counselled Elijah on making a strategic retreat after His Word of the prophecy of drought for three years. He was sustained in the desert with water from the brook at Terebinth and with meat and bread brought to him by ravens. He overcame his fear of the power of King

46. Leaders are Climate Changers

Ahab and his wicked queen Jezebel. When the widow of Zarephath cried out for her son's life, Elijah resurrected the child by lying on his dead body. When Elijah offered a sacrifice, the Lord sent down fire to consume his offering. The Lord vindicated the words of Elijah's mouth and proved it to be His own. We, too, might be ordinary people like Elijah in terms of our background or where we come from, but the Lord has called us to be extraordinary. When the Word of the Lord is constantly in our mouths and on our minds, He will anoint us with sustaining power, we do not have to worry over what we will eat or drink even during a time of famine.

The Lord will provide for our needs. He will give us overcoming power to speak the Word with authority as Elijah did. He will give us overwhelming power against our mortal foes and enemies. He will give us wonder-working power. He will not let a word from our mouths fall to the ground without being fulfilled. He will cause miracles to happen that will manifest His awesome power. He will give us power over the elements of nature, to command the rain to cease and to fall. Our sacrifices will be acceptable and pleasing to the Lord. The powers manifested in our lives are not to draw attention to us but to point people to God. There were different seasons in Elijah's walk with God. He was willing to stand up for God and speak on His behalf the uncompromising Word.

Therefore, the Lord chose to honour him and His Words. The climax of Elijah's leadership was his being taken away in a chariot of fire. Elijah was a king-shaker, king-remover and king-anointer. He did not forecast the weather but caused it. Many world leaders at the UN met to focus on the phenomenon of climate change. Elijah was the cause of climate change. God chose to establish him and His Word as He establishes us and our words in this day and time. He wants us to be climate changers like Elijah in the 21st century. Like the widow at Zarephath and the people of Israel and King Ahab were witnesses of the extraordinary presence and power of God with Elijah, the least to the greatest in the land we dwell in, will be witnesses to the presence and power of God in our lives.

47. DESTINED FOR LEADERSHIP

> "THE LORD HATH BEEN MINDFUL OF US, HE WILL BLESS US, HE WILL BLESS THE HOUSE OF ISRAEL AND HE WILL BLESS THE HOUSE OF AARON."
>
> – **Psalms 115:12**

The Lord has His mind full of us and our well-being. He is ever conscious of us. He is aware of our names, our needs and our challenges. His intellect is focused on plans for our well-being and future. His emotions are centered on our happiness. His decisions, actions and interventions are fixed on securing His will and desire for our lives. He is preoccupied with our present joy, future hope and eternal destiny. From His perspective, the eternal outweighs the past, present and future. This is the reason He allows a measure of suffering and trials in the lives of His chosen. Nothing in history or science or the contemporary compares with the value of the eternal. The price to live forever in the presence of God is very high and cannot be paid for by a man's good deeds or by following certain rites, rules and rituals.

It was paid for in full by His Son Jesus. He gave us this right to be part of Israel or the commonwealth of Israel and gave us the key of David, faith to enter therein. The blessing on David's forefather Abraham was passed on to us by faith. We use the key of David to enter the house of Israel and to have a personal relationship with God. Now it is our turn to be mindful of God. Only a true priest of God is always mindful of Him. We are to move from just being a believer of Jehovah or Elijah to being part of the house of Aaron: a closer bonding with the Lord dedicated and serving the Lord. We are called to continually worship the Lord, to intercede for those who have not yet entered the house of Israel. We exist not for our own pleasure but the pleasure of the Lord.

Our own blessings and rewards are like meat for the sustenance of the worker. When we fulfill our onus or our responsibilities as a priest, He gives us a bonus, or what is good for us and our families. He gives us the anointing He gave Aaron and the anointing He gave David. We need to have the heart of sacrifice of a priest and the reverence for God that a priest has. God is our employer. He pays our wages. We need to have the strength, boldness and courage of a king like David. The Lord's ear is always open to our prayers and cries of our hearts. He hears us even before we pray or a word is uttered from our mouths. He will bless us as He blessed Israel and as He blessed Aaron and his generations. The blessings of Israel are listed in the first fourteen verses of Deuteronomy 28. We are blessed wherever we are.

We do not have to go in search of any place or person in pursuit of blessing. We are destined for an increase. We are destined for safekeeping and security. We are destined for success in everything we do. We are destined

47. Destined for Leadership

for holiness. We are destined for true and blessed fame and true riches. We are destined to rule. We are destined for leadership and primacy. For these aspects of our destiny to be fulfilled and for our heritage to be claimed and enjoyed, we ought to be mindful of the commands and enthusiastic in believing and claiming the promises of God. We are destined to be in the presence of the Lord and to serve Him and His people. Our life will not be without struggles, but instead of struggling with God, we will only hereafter struggle with our common enemy and those of our own kind. Like Israel, we will be surrounded by enemies of different kinds and few faithful friends. Like Joseph, we might be betrayed by our own brothers. Like Jesus, we might be let down by our own but each trial and struggle will make us better and not bitter for He is with us as Immanuel and Ebenezer. He will fight for us and give us testimonies out of all our tests and trials.

48. LEADERSHIP AND THE POWER TO BLESS

"BLESS THE LORD, O MY SOUL AND ALL THAT IS WITHIN ME, BLESS HIS HOLY NAME."

– Psalms 103:1

The power to bless is associated with divinity. Yet, how did David dare to bless the Lord? It is on account of the divinity that dwells in every child of God that we can bless the Lord. David commanded his own soul to bless the Lord. To bless implies to lift up, to enlarge, to exalt, to cause good to happen. The Lord does not need man's help. Yet, He feels gratified when we bless Him. He will not repent for having created us and thereafter, redeemed us with Jesus. We are called to be leaders who are a blessing to the world and not a curse or a burden. If we have the power to bless God, then how much more do we have the power and responsibility to bless those whom we are leading or serving or teaching! The important thing to note is that we do not bless in our own right but the name of the Lord.

David goes on to direct all that is within him to bless the holy name of God. What lies within us includes all of our faculties, all of our organs, all of our plans and visions, all of our achievements and failures, all of our memories and all of our desires and hopes. The American philosopher

48. Leadership and the Power to Bless

Ralph Waldo Emerson wrote, "What lies behind us and what lies before us are tiny matters compared to what lies within us." This is not necessarily true but when read and lived in conjunction with our faith in the living God, then what lies ahead of us and what lies behind us will become tiny matters. The word "holy" also means holistic. We need to bless people in all dimensions of life and not just appeal to their intellectual or emotional faculties.

Without factoring in God, how can we understand life? Without understanding life, how can we come up with an adequate response to our challenges? We need to bless the Lord's name with all of our best, our faculties, our conscience, our dreams, our desires, hopes, thoughts, emotions, imagination, talents, wisdom, knowledge and understanding. Since we are called to be His own, we are also called after the Lord's name. With all these resources and abilities and potential that lie within us, we need to bring glory to the Lord's name. The means we adopt to achieve our goals should bring glory to His name. Our ambitions and goals should bring glory to His name. David went to battle the giant Goliath with inadequate training, inadequate experience and inadequate weapons but he went with abundant faith that made up for every inadequacy. He went in the name of His Lord and God, in the name of the God of Israel.

That testimony is a blessing for all generations and a blessing to the name of the Lord. The Tabernacle or temple of ancient Israel had many parts with different functions and purposes but the ultimate purpose was to worship and glorify God. Similarly, all that lies within us is meant to glorify or bless the name of the Lord. Our desire to provide for ourselves and our families is something placed in us by God. It is blessed by Him. Our efforts to do so will bless the Jireh dimension of His name. Our desire to be channels of peace and to be problem solvers blesses the Shalom dimension of His name. Our desire for wisdom and counsel is blessed by the Rohi or Shepherd dimension of His name.

Our triumphs and victories over trials, tribulations and persecution bless the Nissi dimension of His name. The healing that we pray for ourselves and others blesses the Rapha dimension of His name. When we deal with our own inner weaknesses and the pulls and pressures to yield to external temptations or to conform to the world instead of His Word, we are blessing the El Shaddai dimension of the name of God. Every exercise of faith blesses or lifts up the name of the Lord. When we use every talent and gift we have been endowed with and utilise every opportunity we are given, we are blessing the name of the Lord.

49. METAMORPHIC LEADERSHIP

"HE SAITH UNTO THEM, FOLLOW ME AND I WILL MAKE YOU FISHERS OF MEN."

– **Matthew 4:19**

Other leaders ask their followers to follow them and keep them as followers all their lives while Jesus alone said, "Come and follow me and I will make you" a positive influence in the world, a leader, a leader of leaders, a leader-maker, a holistic leader, a truthful leader, a trained and discipled leader and a leader into eternity. He makes them too. It is metamorphic leadership. Instead of working for the mundane and perishable fishes and loaves of office or vocation, Jesus shifts the paradigm of leadership and management to a higher plane. This is the difference between a mere vocation and a calling. A calling meets an inner urge and an outward vision or a call of God. Instead, of working for men, we work for God. God will pay our wages or provide what is needed for our sustenance. Our perspective is transformed from the temporal and transient to the eternal.

When Jesus said, "Follow me..", He did not mean only physically but to follow what He says, to follow what He did and to follow Him where He went. The tracks of other leaders end at their graves but Jesus left a trail into eternity to follow Him into the Father's mansion. The disciple's journey begins and ends in Jesus. He does not lead us anywhere for He Himself is the commencer and finisher, He Himself is the way, the truth and the life. Jesus shows us that we need not feed fish to people or even teach them fishing but we only need to induce in them a belief that they too can fish or that they too can be saved and lead others to salvation. Jesus recognised that the greatest need of mankind is not food but salvation. The function of spiritual leadership is to point people to their salvation. A fisherman relies on his nets to catch fish while a leader depends on his network.

He spreads his positive influence in the lives of people like salt spreads its flavour through an entire meal- invisibly, silently and without much fanfare. A fisherman always focuses on the day's catch while a leader focuses on the impact of his whole life. Fishermen work in teams and seldom solo. Similarly, leaders need to work in teams. Fishermen are never contented catching a single fish or a few but they aim for abundance. Similarly, leaders aim to impact an abundant number of people. The fisherman image can be extended to various professions in the contemporary world. If one is a physician, he now becomes through the call of Jesus a divine physician. If he is a police officer, he now becomes a watchman for the Lord. If a teacher, a teacher for the Lord. If a home-maker, a home-maker and keeper for the Lord.

There is another implication of the fisherman metaphor, people without faith and hope in a living and

49. Metamorphic Leadership

loving God, without hope of living forever in fellowship with the Creator and Redeemer are like fish lying on the shore struggling for oxygen even though there is plenty of oxygen in the atmosphere. It is a strange case of "oxygen, oxygen everywhere but not a molecule to breathe." The oxygen needs to be mixed in water for the fish to breathe through its gills. Similarly, hope is plentifully mixed or dissolved in the Word. People need to be taught to swim in this living water instead of struggling and being desperate on dry land. Just as a fisherman needs to have certain natural strength, stamina, skills and discipline in order to fish successfully, in order to lead successfully, we need to use our natural gifts, skills and talents diligently, consistently and perseveringly.

In the post-resurrection phase, Jesus again calls the disciples back from what seemed like a failed fishing trip by leading them into outstanding success and enabling them to catch abundant fish. So much so, the nets were filled to the tearing point. Now their real calling as apostles to the world began. Similarly, outstanding success by divine enablement in our professions is not a confirmation that our calling is over or fulfilled but it might just be the beginning of a higher and deeper work of the Lord in and through our lives.

50. BE A STAR LEADER

> "THEY THAT BE WISE SHALL SHINE AS THE BRIGHTNESS OF THE FIRMAMENT AND THEY THAT TURN MANY TO RIGHTEOUSNESS AS THE STARS FOREVER AND EVER."
>
> **– Daniel 12:3**

Leadership is not just influence but positive influence. The influence comes from wisdom and righteousness and not power or position or ability and accomplishment. Just as the stars declare the glory of God in the skies, godly leaders declare the glory of God on earth among mankind. Though there are a trillion stars in the universe, not one is exactly the same as the other. Leaders are stars in the eyes of the Lord, each a shining example forever and each unique and set apart. A leader by definition leads people out of darkness, ignorance of God and His Word into His light and truth, into personal knowledge of the One who not only created us but redeemed us. The Book of Proverbs defines the wise as those who win souls for the Kingdom of God. Leaders who do not invest their lives in an everlasting purpose are like fireflies that glow with some transient glory.

Leaders are not worried about excessive or gross darkness in the world. They act as peacemakers, pace-setters and problem-solvers. The greater the darkness, the stars

50. Be a Star Leader

shine to light up the sky. The stars and their formations are the ancient compasses set in the sky for earthly sojourners to navigate their paths. Similarly, leaders help people navigate their lives and reach their divine destination. They become the cause and stimulus for changing the direction of people's lives. Worldly leaders are set apart by their worldly knowledge, scientific, literary, economic or political, but godly leaders are set apart not by knowledge but by wisdom. The stars are an almost inexhaustible source of power and energy. Similarly, godly leaders have access to infinite power and energy.

Their influence or light cuts through great distances and deep darkness. Just as stars have an orbit, leaders have certain positions and orbits in which the Lord has set them. They give out more light than they take. The wise have a head star-t. They think ahead of priorities and focus on these. It implies that they start by allowing the Lord to touch and transform their thoughts, temperament, tongue, talent and time. They point people to Jesus who is the way, the truth and the life. They know they have no righteousness of their own and that it is the finished work of Jesus on the cross that makes them righteous in the eyes of the Lord.

They build their lives and leadership on the solid rock principles embedded in the eternal Word of God and not the changing ideas, whims and thoughts of human beings. Though they develop amazing power and impact, they withdraw themselves to the background of the skies to remain tiny twinkling dots. They bow before the Sun of Righteousness and bask in His glory. Right through history, numerous leaders in different fields including Newton and Edison have left their shining examples as star leaders who are bright, wise and righteous. In biblical times, Daniel and his three companions were star leaders. They excelled as much in saying, "No" to certain things as they said "Yes" to God. They subjected themselves to disciplining their appetite for the world and cultivating their taste for things of eternal value. They took a principled stand against the high and mighty of the land and were courageous enough to be willing to pay the price for it. They continue to inspire faith, hope, courage and integrity in succeeding generations of people of nationalities around the world while the memory of the great kings they served has only become faded or been cited as examples of negative leadership or negative influence.

51. EAGLE-LIKE LEADERSHIP

"AS AN EAGLE STIRRETH UP HER NEST, FLUTTERETH OVER HER YOUNG, SPREADETH ABROAD HER WINGS, TAKETH THEM, BEARETH THEM ON HER WINGS."

– **Deuteronomy 31:11**

*A*n eagle is one of the strongest as well as most regal of birds. Though it is known for its ruthlessness with its prey, it is extremely caring as a parent to its young. The eagle has a long life of almost a human life span of seventy years. Its wings are long and powerful. It can instantly move up to great heights and remain afloat close to the clouds. It is tireless. It is focused on its objectives whether to obtain prey or to train its young to fly. The eagle's eye expression implies that nothing escapes the attention of the eagle even as it hovers high above. The eagle makes its nest on the mountain cliff. Once the young eaglets are ready for flight in the judgment of the mother eagle, the eagle stirs its nest or disturbs it so that the young ones are forced to learn to fly.

The parent eagle hovers over and catches the young on its pinions should they fall perilously down the cliff. Initially, the young eaglets go hurtling down the cliff before they pick up the strength and courage to flap their own wings and attempt to fly.

In life and leadership, the Lord God deals with mankind as the mother eagle deals with its young. Apparently, the eagle cares for the eaglets and does not want the young to stay longer than necessary in the comfort of the nest. The eagle nudges the eaglets to venture to the edge of the nest and stirs or disturbs the soft upper layers of the nest so that the thorns and thistles in the lower levels make the nest even less comfortable and inviting to stay. Eaglets are born to fly or have the inherent capacity to fly high in the skies. Even so, we are born to lead. God has intended that every child of His discovers and fulfils his or her full potential. He hovers over us as we learn to live and lead even as the mother eagle looks out for other predators and threats to the lives of the eaglets.

Once the eaglets have learnt to fly and are confident, the mother eagle moves away so that they too can form their own nest and have their own young. At times in its life, the eagle stays on the cliff and shed all its feathers and begins to grow new ones. Similarly, we too should return to the Lord and renew our strength, renew our hope, faith and joy. The Lord will bear us on the wings of prayer and the Word. His very shadow or presence in our lives is like a mountain fastness. An eagle is most powerful not when it is resting on a branch of a tree but while it is flying. Similarly, we are most formidable while we are praying, meditating or studying the Word.

The eagle's pinions are the long feathers of its wings. The pinions of the Lord on which He catches us while we are falling from great heights and in mid-flight are His promises. The curved beak and the talons of the eagle

51. Eagle-like Leadership

are its defence against more powerful predators. These are the tough side of our personalities which is seen when we have to take hard or tough decisions at certain points in our lives. The eagle takes its strong foes off the ground, for instance, a serpent is carried into the air where it is helpless against the eagle's tearing beak and claws. A strong leader should also know what his or her advantages are and what strategies to adopt against different adversaries. We are called to be strong as the eagle and gentle as the dove. We are to love our enemies but stay away from their claws and clutches.

52. HEADSHIP AND LEADERSHIP

> "THE BREAKER HAS COME UP BEFORE THEM, THEY HAVE BROKEN UP AND HAVE PASSED THROUGH THE GATE AND ARE GONE OUT BY IT AND THEIR KING SHALL PASS BEFORE THEM AND THE LORD ON THE HEAD OF THEM."
>
> – Micah 2:13

The uni-verse promises that the Lord will go before us as our king and leader. He will break our chains, anything that limits our potential and our growth. He breaks the bondages within us and the barriers and hurdles before us. He sets the prisoners free and gives hope to the hopeless. He gives sight to the blind. We are the blind who do not have a spiritual vision. The Lord imparts an eternal vision so that we see His purpose and His power and experience His grace on a day-to-day basis. The headship of God is as necessary as the eyes for the head of a man. The head thinks of the well-being of the whole body. The head stimulates or moves the different parts of the body, the hidden organs as well as the external limbs to act in the interest of the whole body. These are the roles of leadership. The head cannot exist without the body and the body without the head. They are interdependent. Without the headship of the Lord, we will grope in darkness. We will not know which path to take in our lives.

The Messiah is the one who will open the gate of life and the floodgates of blessings. He has the form of a man but the power of God- one like us and yet sent by God and God Himself. He is both king and servant. He has walked the paths of suffering and truth that He now beckons us to walk. He has gone ahead of us, leaving us both examples and precepts. We only need to diligently follow Him. The opening of a door needs faith for we do not know what lies on the other side. Faith can be either a getaway from life and reality or a gateway to greater freedom, responsibility and fulfilment.

The Lord wants us to make faith in His name and His Word a gateway and not a getaway. He wants us to face reality and not hide or get away from it. Jesus proclaimed Himself as the gate to everlasting life, the door to salvation. He manifests Himself in the life of every believing human being as a solution, an answer, a breakthrough giver. We enter the presence and avail the power of God by entering through this door. Jesus is the one leader in all of history who broke through the limitations of knowledge, of wisdom, of resources, of power in every possible way. He revealed what lay on the other side of the door of death. He is an overcomer and expects us to be an overcomer. He is the One who can give us the breakthroughs we need and expect in life. Every day and every moment is like a gate or a door, an opportunity to experience the grace and power of the leadership of the Lord. Every difficulty and challenge we face is a bronze gate or door that the Lord breaks open for us.

53. THE INNER LAMP OF LEADERSHIP

"SO GIDEON AND THE HUNDRED MEN THAT WERE WITH HIM, CAME UNTO THE OUTSIDE OF THE CAMP IN THE BEGINNING OF THE MIDDLE WATCH AND THEY HAD BUT NEWLY SET THE WATCH AND THEY BLEW THE TRUMPETS AND BRAKE THE PITCHERS THAT WERE IN THEIR HANDS."

– Judges 7:19

Gideon was a leader called and anointed by the Lord. He was an unlikely as well as reluctant leader. He did not expect to be anointed as a leader. He sought confirmation from the Lord that he was indeed called. He was given the details of how to "fight" the Midianites who were superior in number and force. He was asked to go against them with just 300 men who were set apart. Leaders who are set apart by their love for God and a hunger and thirst for righteousness are mightier than the mightiest army. Such leaders are like a lamp burning within the earthen pitcher of their own bodies. Their faith is their trumpet that signals victory. Gideon chose a strategic place and a strategic time to launch his attack.

53. The Inner Lamp of Leadership

He chose the outside of the camp of the Midianites and the beginning of the middle watch when the guards were just about to change. Similarly, leaders should know the strategic times and the strategy that the Lord will give to create change and claim victory over the opposing forces of darkness. The pitchers that were broken are a metaphor for our own inhibitions, fears and limitations that the Lord breaks with His Word. They had no weapons and no military training but were able to put the Midianites to rout and deliver Israel from oppression. The lamp of leadership that gives direction, illumination, warmth and guidance is the Word burning in our minds and hearts. That lamp generates power and victory.

The Lord delivered Israel through the strategy that He gave Gideon. The three hundred men were chosen on the basis of their lapping water like a dog from the hollow of their palms and not by bending down on their knees to drink directly from the river. The water is a metaphor for the Word. These men applied the manna or specific word they received from the Lord, the river of life daily, applied it and received the blessing, anointing and power. The key factor was that the three companies of men Gideon chose acted in unison as led by the Lord. They were faithful and courageous to obey implicitly and follow the leadership of the Lord. They put their lives at risk on account of their confidence in the Lord and Gideon, their divinely anointed leader. Similarly, we need to wait on the Lord for the details of His plan of action and share it with carefully chosen leaders who would implicitly obey the Lord in every detail of His instruction.

54. LEADERSHIP IS HEADSHIP NOT TAILSHIP

"THE LORD SHALL MAKE THEE THE HEAD AND NOT THE TAIL AND THOU SHALT BE ABOVE ONLY AND THOU SHALT NOT BE BENEATH, IF THAT THOU HEARKEN UNTO THE COMMANDMENTS OF THE LORD THY GOD, WHICH I COMMAND THEE THIS DAY, TO OBSERVE AND TO DO THEM."

– Deuteronomy 28:13

"The ancient and honourable is the head while the prophet who teaches lies is the tail" by definition of scripture. God is the head of the universe, the head of heaven and earth and all that is in it and the head of the human family. It is intended that those who follow the Lord be likewise the head and not the tail. The tail is only an appendix that can be cut off or it is dispensable. The tail is a symbol of weak and ineffective leadership. Most of the leaders throughout history have acted as tails when they should have been heads. Those who are strongly committed to the truth are destined to be heads and not tails. It is intended by the Lord that those who follow Him faithfully become leaders of humanity, leaders in

54. Leadership is Headship not Tailship

the nations and leaders in their professions and localities. They shall be "above" pettiness and meanness, above want, above wickedness and corruption.

They shall not come under the shadow of scams and scandals. The only precondition is that they diligently listen, study, meditate, observe, absorb, apply or "do" the commands of the Lord. The words, "This day" implies that our past record of leadership does not count – it is only what we do now. Leadership has the functions of the human head- to see or envision, to think or to look beyond the superficial reality and find the inner meaning of things, the ultimate purpose of life, to find solutions to difficulties, problems and challenges, to expand or grow and develop in positive ways. Leadership has the function of hearing or listening to feedback. It has the function of being the mouthpiece or communicating truths that have been learnt.

Like the head is also the face of a person, a leader is the face of a nation, an organisation, a corporate or a family. Like the face is the index of the heart, the leader reflects the state of the nation or organisation or business. Just as the face breaks into a smile or tears or signs of surprise or anger or indignation, it is the leader's role to motivate, move, inspire and cheer up the followers. Just as the head is the crown of the human body, the leader is the one who bears the responsibility as well as honour. Just as the head turns on the neck, the leader is the one who takes the nation, the organisation or the business in new directions, initiatives and course corrections. He is the direction finder, the one who determines and decides what paths the nation or organisation needs to take. The leader is the one who plans ahead of time to fulfilling the needs of the whole body. The leader is the one who imagines and dreams.

He is the one who takes steps for the protection, safety and security of the whole being or whole organisation. The head feeds the whole body but it does not retain the entire nourishment but sees that it is equitably distributed to the different parts. Similarly, leaders should not be avaricious and try to corner all the gains or collect all the wealth for their own use but distribute it proportionately according to the varied needs of the followers. The glands for growth are located in the head – so likewise, a leader should plan for the growth of the entire nation, organisation or business to take it to the next level. The head plans for rest, recreation and recuperation of the body at appropriate times. So also leaders need to provide for breaks, relaxation and recovery of followers.

The head is the hardest or strongest part of the human skeleton. It protects the softest and most valuable part of the body, that is, the brain. Similarly, leaders need to be strong to endure the toughest times and challenges, but they need to be soft and compassionate internally or at their heart level. Leadership is eventually a fine combination of hard and soft skills and strategies. We got to be hard in the hard areas and soft in the soft areas. Just as the head is the pivot of the body, Christ is the head of the church, a body of believers in His vision, mission and passion. As leaders, we are expected to imitate or emulate Him in how He gave up all the privileges of heaven to come to the earth

54. Leadership is Headship not Tailship

in a humble form and how He ministered or served people in a variety of need situations and finally, gave Himself up for the well-being of humanity. Even today, instead of judging people, He acts as an intercessor and mediator before and besides the Father's throne. We, too as leaders called and anointed by Christ should not judge but help others achieve their potential to be heads and not tails.

55. THE LEADERSHIP TREE

"THE BRAMBLE SAID UNTO THE TREES, 'IF IN TRUTH YE ANOINT ME KING OVER YOU, THEN COME AND PUT YOUR TRUST IN MY SHADOW AND IF NOT, LET FIRE COME OUT OF THE BRAMBLE AND DEVOUR THE CEDARS OF LEBANON.'"

– Judges 9:15

*J*otham's parable on the "bramble of leadership" is a wonderful lesson on leadership relevant to modern times as it was at the time he spoke it. Jotham was comparing the leadership of Abimelech, his stepbrother and son of Gideon as nothing but bramble or a thorn bush whose fire would one day destroy all other trees even as he had killed seventy of the sons of Gideon. The trees, implying the people of their tribe and clan went out to select or elect a leader and ended up selecting the bramble or the thorn bush. They ignored the claims to leadership of the tallest among them in beauty and character, the cedars. They ignored the godly leaders, the anointed of God, chosen to serve God and man, the olive trees whose leaves symbolised peace and whose fruit gave nourishment, good for the human heart and spirit, yielding pure oil that would act as a lubricant, medicine, an excellent cooking medium.

They did not even choose the fig tree whose fruit was sweet and healthy. They did not choose the vine, the vine

55. The Leadership Tree

that had no strength to stand on its own and needed props but stayed humble and close to the ground or reality. A leader should be like a tree in enabling people to climb up to their full potential using its branches. Leadership like a tree should be fruitful. A leader should be a source of blessing to those he leads. External charisma is not the criterion. Very often the most charismatic leaders lack the moral courage or inner character to be an example to their followers. The vanity and charm of the physically charismatic and the highly talented delude them into thinking that they have a natural right to lord it over others and that leadership is a privilege that they were born into. These are the cedars of leadership, the cedar has a beauty, stature and fragrance of its wood that makes it stand out as the natural king among trees.

What distinguishes the different types of leaders? Their seed or source of inspiration is different. Their root or what they derive their support and strength from is different. Their branches or parts of their lives are different. Their sap or source of motivation is different. Their leaves or words and thoughts are different. The very wind or influence to which they sway is different. Their fragrance or invisible aura is different. When we scour the pages of world and national history, we find all these types of trees of leadership. The olive tree leaders were few: Nelson Mandela, Mother Teresa, M.K. Gandhi and the greatest of olive tree leaders, Jesus Himself. The bramble of leaders were many, Napoleon, Hitler, Stalin, Mao and so on. The fire of their fierce ambition and ruthlessness destroyed thousands upon thousands.

Leaders who do not have any other goal but to perpetuate and promote themselves and their families at the expense of the organisation or nation are the bramble, the thorn bushes who are ready to hurt or harm others to advance their own cause. The bramble is envious of the cedars and the olive tree leaders and would gladly set these on fire to eliminate any possible future competition. They lack vision as well as passion and mission. A mission is a larger-than-life purpose for which one is ready to make any sacrifice and if needed one's own life. Such bramble leaders have marked themselves for self-destruction as most of the tyrants, dictators and despots of history have through the generations. Non-charismatic but principled and godly leaders are the "olive tree" leaders who exist for a larger and nobler purpose. They seek not to enrich themselves but to enlarge, ennoble and enable others to live a better life.

These are leaders who like olive trees endure for long, whose memories and example outlive their own lives. People crush or analyse their words like olive fruit is crushed in the olive press to derive meaning and power. They stay evergreen or passionate and consistent about their vision, passion and mission in life. Though they are exalted to high positions, their attitude is one of being a servant to many people and to the One Almighty God. They derive their strength and nourishment from the anointing Word, spirit and wisdom of the Lord.

56. THE HOLY GROUND OF LIFE AND LEADERSHIP

"HE SAID, 'DRAW NOT NIGH HITHER, PUT OFF THY SHOES FROM OFF THY FEET, FOR THE PLACE WHEREON THOU STANDEST IS HOLY GROUND.'"

– **Exodus 3:5**

Where the presence of the Lord is, that is "holy ground". The presence of the Lord is everywhere to which and to whom He is invited and honoured. Hence, all of the earth is holy ground in that sense. No place is "God forsaken". No person is "God forsaken." Leadership and positions of authority are holy ground as persons in leadership are appointed, anointed and chosen by the specific knowledge and consent of the Lord. Hence, no one should go rushing into areas of leadership but wait on the Lord to find His will and purpose, obtain His grace and power, wisdom and leading before wearing the mantle of leadership. There should not be any arrogant display of power. As it is said, "One can have the power of a giant but he should not use it like one." A leader should be a person who is conscientious and accountable to God and man. He should not take his duties lightly or his privileges for granted. Leadership is meant to serve and not to be served. The more people we serve and the more ways we serve them, the greater is our calling.

The concept of leadership and life itself being "holy ground" should produce a sense of reverence for the Lord in us. That sense of awe and respect for the Lord will in turn engender the wisdom that will keep us from committing wilful blunders or folly. An unwanted thought, an unwanted gesture, an unwanted word could offend the Lord and this uni-verse teaches us to guard against anything that offends the Lord.

Moses under the old covenant relationship with the Lord could not draw near to the presence of the Lord but we are called by our names and are expected to draw nearer and nearer to the Lord. A similar 'holy ground' experience during the transfiguration of Jesus in the company of Moses and Elijah got Peter all excited and he offered to build three tabernacles for them. All Peter had to do was to offer his life and his body as the tabernacle of the Lord. Our bodies are on holy ground when we offer ourselves as a tabernacle for Lord and the indwelling Holy Spirit takes control of our lives.

"Putting off the shoes" is a metaphor to deal with anything in us and around us that defiles and offends the Lord. We need to put off our worries, our pride, our lusts and our fears as we draw near to the Lord. The shoes are also a symbol of whatever is made by the hands of man including man-made religion and ritual. We cannot come to the Lord on the strength of anything we are or we have done. We can approach His holiness or perfection only by virtue of His grace and mercy. We need to completely focus on the Lord and appreciate the beauty of His holiness, the depth of His love and the extent of His power, grace

56. The Holy Ground of Life and Leadership

and mercy. Ultimately and immediately, as we do so, we become the holy ground of the presence of the Lord, the living temples sanctified by Jesus. The transformation is striking, from a position of awe and reverence, of distance and fear we move in our spirits to a position of intimacy and complete identification with the Lord. The Lord then lights not a bush that does not burn down but He lights the fire in our bellies, a passion and zeal to exceed and excel for His glory. By the power of the Holy Spirit, we burn brightly but we do not get consumed.

57. LEADERSHIP TRAITS

> "MOREOVER THOU SHALT PROVIDE OUT OF ALL THE PEOPLE ABLE MEN, SUCH AS FEAR GOD, MEN OF TRUTH, HATING COVETOUSNESS AND PLACE SUCH OVER THEM, TO BE RULERS OF THOUSANDS, RULERS OF HUNDREDS, RULERS OF FIFTIES AND RULERS OF TENS."
>
> – **Exodus 18:21**

Whether a person is the captain of a small boat or a big ship, the rules of navigation of leadership remain the same. He needs to chart the course for the vessel to reach the port of destination. He needs to provide supplies for the crew. He has to take steps for the security of the vessel. He has to maintain discipline on board. He has to plan and be ready for contingencies and emergencies. Above all, he should know the direction in which he should sail. He should have a compass or GPS to guide him. The complexity might increase but the rules and principles of leadership remain the same. Jethro underlined the basic principles of leadership. The ability to lead, rule, govern and judge is a given.

It is a basic consideration to choose people to occupy positions of leadership, but more fundamentally, they should possess qualities and attitudes of fear of God, integrity and hatred, not mere dislike, of covetousness.

57. Leadership Traits

The fear of God is the fountainhead of wisdom, of values in actual practice as against mere advocacy or professing to possess the values. A person with the ability of a high order but without the fear of God will become a law unto himself once he is clothed with authority over others. He does not hold himself accountable to those he leads. He is filled with pride and arrogance. He begins to exploit those he leads instead of serving them. If he fears God and knows he is accountable not just for every action or reaction but for every word and even thought or emotion, he will correct himself whenever he goes wrong.

If he is a believer, he will be sensitive to the whispers and promptings of the Holy Spirit and walk in the path of righteousness indicated by the Holy Spirit. All the systems of man and attempts to prevent and often even detect and punish corruption in all nations have failed in keeping the leaders on the straight and narrow. A person who fears the Lord loves the truth hidden in His Word and learns to cherish and treasure it more than necessary food. He will be diligent in unearthing the truth and abiding by it. Even if he fails or falls, he will rise up every time and try to avoid the pitfalls of leadership. Those who neither know the truth nor have a desire to know it are like the blind leading the blind.

They appear to lead but do not know where they are heading. They are like a ship without a rudder or helm. They will fall into the pits of untruth and unrighteousness and lead many others also into it. A person who loves the truth will hate dishonest gain and injustice. The principles of life and leadership that underline every uni-verse steer them and lead them through the storms of life. He derives his vision from his values. He knows where he is going and where he is leading the led. He is deeply anchored in the values that give him the strength and courage to face the high seas of life. He is never insecure as his faith in the Lord keeps him grounded and on an even keel at the best and worst of times.

58. THE LIGHT OF LEADERSHIP

"THERE SHALL BE NO NIGHT THERE AND THEY NEED NO CANDLE, NEITHER LIGHT OF THE SUN, FOR THE LORD GOD GIVETH THEM LIGHT AND THEY SHALL REIGN FOREVER AND EVER."

– **Revelations 22:5**

God is light and in Him is no darkness, neither ignorance nor evil. He gives us His light, love, integrity, goodness, godliness, grace, happiness, holiness, health, truth, tenacity and triumph over darkness or evil. The absence of God is evil. The absence of goodness is evil or darkness. The presence of God brings light. People living in darkness get used to it and do not want to experience light. They do not understand light or acquire these qualities. These are the spiritual graces that distinguish a godly leader. The path of each of these factors becomes brighter and brighter and does not diminish. We need to increase the measure of our love for God and our fellow man. We need to increase our understanding of the love of God and discern its unfathomable depth, its length, and width.

Love is three-dimensional even as life is three-dimensional. It implies that our love should be manifested in real-time in a real way. Unlike God who is absolute in all these attributes or graces, we need to keep increasing in each quality, in love, integrity, goodness, godliness, grace, happiness, holiness, holistic health, truth, tenacity and triumph over the forces and factors of darkness. Light travels far and fast. Similarly, these godly attributes of ours, given to us by grace, need to travel far and fast for His glory. The Lord has intended each of us to be a leader in our own rights but by His light. He desires that we be the head and not the tail. He desires that we be visionary leaders and not blind or short-sighted leaders. The span of our vision should extend to eternity and the width should cover the whole globe. He anoints us as rulers or leaders. Except for the house of leadership not being built in vain, the ruler's labour would be in vain.

The Lord will help us integrate our spirits, minds and bodies such that we have a sense of integrity and we experience oneness with Him. He will show us His goodness. He will add grace to grace in our lives. He will shape our character to be godly or like Him. He will cause us and teach us to be happy, peaceful or blessed as defined by Jesus in the Sermon on the Mount. He will sanctify us and rid us of all hidden factors that contaminate our faith and lives. He will reveal the hidden truths in His Word so that we can judge ourselves in accordance with it and set right our areas of error and falsehood.

We need no human teachers or blind leaders to lead us for the Spirit of God Himself will guide us into all truth and teach us all that we need to know. We become the channels to usher in the rule of God on earth. We subject

58. The Light of Leadership

ourselves to His discipline. We exercise authority over the spiritual realms in His name and on His behalf. We shall overcome the world even as Jesus overcame the world. He has anointed us to reign as kings and priests, kings in authority over the spiritual realms and the invisible world and priests to intercede on behalf of fellow believers and the lost and spiritually blind.

We have to blend or balance firmness with compassion, authority with humility and exercise our spiritual gifts with diligence. We need to be consistent in manifesting or celebrating by experiencing love, integrity, goodness, grace, godliness, happiness, holiness, holistic health and truthfulness. Our choice at best be a lesser or greater degree of each of these attitudes and attributes. Our aim should be an ever-increasing degree. Our endeavour should be not to allow an alternation between light and darkness, between love and hatred, integrity and dishonesty, goodness and evil, happiness and sadness, holiness and a lack of reverence for God, truth and its absence or violation. Darkness can never resist the light. It flees in the presence of light. Hence, when we experience and cherish the light, the dark factors of our lives that troubled us this far shall flee.

59. THE SERVANT LEADER VERSUS THE SERPENT LEADER

"OF THE TREE OF THE KNOWLEDGE OF GOOD AND EVIL, THOU SHALT NOT EAT OF IT, FOR IN THE DAY THAT THOU EATEST THEREOF THOU SHALT SURELY DIE."

– **Genesis 2:17**

Knowledge of good and evil has made mankind a mixture. God created mankind to multiply and dominate or lead the earth with the knowledge of good only initially, but satan, the serpent leader led man to disbelieve God and discredit His goodness, to scorn His grace, to reject His authority and come under the authority of the enemy of our souls. Historically, two lines of human leadership flow, one from the serpent or satan, the serpent leader, the demagogue, subtle, lying and deceiving and the other, from Jesus, the shepherd king, the servant leader, the pedagogue.

Jesus and Hitler showed us differing models of dissemination, one of truth, the other of untruth, one of love, the other of hatred, the one, a Jew who rose above all sense of nationality, the other a Jew-baiter and hater, one

59. The Servant Leader versus the Serpent Leader

spoke and acted with humility, kindness and mercy, the other with anger and violence and cruelty, the one invested in a dozen lives, the other intimidated millions, the one continues to influence generations, the other fizzled out in a generation. Moral, do not look for a million followers on Twitter or likes on Facebook. Invest in a few with humility, love and kindness and retain influence for generations.

The contrast between different world leaders and the style and content of the leadership of Jesus, the servant leader is illustrative. Napoleon Bonaparte is one such serpent leader. People became the fodder or ammunition for his ambition to dominate Europe and the world. He sacrificed the lives of thousands upon thousands of soldiers to achieve his goals. Like satan who grasped for the crown that belonged to God and unlike Jesus who gave up His crown of Deity to become an ordinary human being, Napoleon hailing from a middle-class family kept climbing the ladder of success and personal ambition, adding title to title till he claimed to be Emperor and grabbing the crown from the Pope, placed it on his own head.

The leaders of the Russian Revolution, Lenin and Stalin were also instances of serpent leaders though they claimed to be servants of the proletariat or the working class. Stalin particularly was extremely despotic and had even his rival Trotsky assassinated. He also organised pogroms or massacres of a large number of dissidents and those who seemed to be a threat to his own power and position. In this context, Mao Tse-tung the leader of Communist China was an example of a serpent leader.

Examples of servant leaders are M.K. Gandhi, Mother Teresa and the young Nobel peace prize winner Malala. These servant leaders were selfless and fearless. They were willing to pay a huge personal price in standing for certain ideals and values. They did not value power or position or titles for their own sake. The exercise of the power of the office is modulated and shaped by some principles that they hold dear to their heart. Abraham Lincoln was one such servant leader who was prepared to sacrifice his life in order to have slavery abolished in the USA. Serpent leaders have some diametrically opposite qualities to servant leaders. The servant leader avoids violence to achieve his or her ends. The serpent leader is like the fox-like Prince of Machiavelli. Passions predominate over principles and values in the case of serpent leaders.

The serpent leader is easily moved by passions like jealousy to take extreme positions and actions. A good example is Cain, the son of Adam who slew his brother Abel out of an early instance of sibling rivalry. A servant leader is compassionate towards those who are less fortunate or underprivileged and takes practical steps to help them in whatever way they can. A serpent leader pretends to be empathetic but it is only a posture he or she takes in order to capture or retain power. A person can start as a serpent leader but be transformed into a servant leader. Emperor Ashoka of the Mauryan dynasty who came to the throne after shedding the blood of a large number of his own kin became a servant leader governed by Buddhist morality after the massacre leading to his victory over the kingdom of Kalinga. He eschewed war as an instrument of

59. The Servant Leader versus the Serpent Leader

state policy thereafter and engaged in a variety of peaceful activities.

Some leaders combine the qualities of a serpent leader and those of a servant leader. John F Kennedy, the President of the USA in the early sixties was an advocate for peace and progress. He stood up to the aggressive postures of the serpent leader Khruschev with firmness and courage. He advocated against racial segregation of the Afro- American people. In his personal life, his sexual peccadillos however detracted from his integrity and legacy and marked him out with some aspects of a serpent leader. Different biblical, as well as contemporary leaders, have demonstrated qualities from time to time of both being a servant leader and a serpent leader. Abraham proved that he was a servant leader when he trusted and obeyed God in attempting to sacrifice his only begotten son even as God sacrificed His only begotten Son Jesus, but Abraham lied about Sarah being his sister in order to stave off the threat from a jealous Pharaoh for his wife was beautiful and would be coveted by the mighty Pharaoh.

Much later Peter lied about not knowing Jesus when he was accused of being His follower as Jesus was being tried before His crucifixion. George Bush in contemporary times lied about Iraq being in possession of nuclear weapons in order to find an excuse to launch an invasion of Iraq to topple Saddam Hussein. Judas Iscariot another disciple of Jesus betrayed His master for thirty silver coins and identified Him to the Pharisees and Roman soldiers with a traitor's kiss. Peter got a second chance to become a servant of Jesus while Judas denied himself the opportunity and died a serpent leader hanging on a rope from a tree in the Potter's field. A servant leader does not take his life or death into his own hands but patiently waits for the Lord to shape him and mould him.

Moses in his early days was a serpent leader. His anger and pride provoked him to kill an Egyptian who was oppressing a fellow Jew, but later he humbled himself as a servant leader. His spirit was broken and he was ready to serve Jehovah. A servant leader serves God in whatever task or role he is assigned or finds himself in. A serpent leader manipulates to achieve his own agenda of domination, of aggrandisement, of deception, of self-gratification.

60. THE ACCOUNTABILITY AND SOURCE OF LEADERSHIP

"HE THAT SPEAKETH OF HIMSELF SEEKETH HIS OWN GLORY, BUT HE THAT SEEKETH HIS GLORY THAT SENT HIM, THE SAME IS TRUE AND NO UNRIGHTEOUSNESS IS IN HIM."

– John 7:18

The serpent leader does everything for his or her own glory and benefit. The servant leader does everything for the glory of God. Jesus said and did everything for the glory of the Father in heaven. He, though being part of the Trinity and God in Himself, held Himself accountable to the Father and the Holy Spirit. The serpent leader in contrast does things on his own, with no sense of accountability. The source of power and influence of the servant leader is not his own self, his own abilities, his own personality, his own ideology, ideas or vision. The source of power and influence is God Himself. The source of power and influence of the serpent leader is his own charisma, his own talents, abilities, ideas and vision.

The servant leader is in continuous fellowship or union with the Father and the Holy Spirit. The serpent leader is averse to any link with the Father or the Holy Spirit. The servant leader is as a consequence, wise, humble and gentle. The serpent leader is foolish, arrogant, proud, rude and violent. The serpent leader exalts himself and is humbled. The servant leader humbles himself and is exalted by God. The serpent leader is conceited and thinks too highly of himself. He speaks often of himself. The servant leader is the messenger of the Lord. He speaks with the authority God has given him. He knows he owes everything he has received to God. He is ever grateful and gracious. The servant leader speaks and seeks the glory of God. The serpent leader seeks and speaks of his own glory. The servant leader has the mind of Christ. He neither deceives nor is deceived. He pours out his life as an offering to God and a blessing to others. His foremost goal is to serve God and man in the highest, deepest and widest way he can. He does not ask, "What is in it for me?" but he constantly asks, "What can I do for others?"

61. A RULER AFTER GOD'S HEART

"THAT I GAVE MY BROTHER HANANI AND HANANIAH THE RULER OF THE PALACE, CHARGE OVER JERUSALEM, FOR HE WAS A FAITHFUL MAN, HE FEARED GOD ABOVE MANY."

– Nehemiah 7:2

People who fear God are likely to be wise rulers. They will have the heart of a servant and a shepherd. They remain humble and diligent. Their faithfulness to God will keep them from being either negligent or corrupt. They would certainly render unto Caesar what is Caesar's, to the people what belongs to them and to God what belongs to God. It is not the most capable or efficient who make the best administrators and rulers but the most faithful ones for the Lord would endow them with wisdom, knowledge, understanding, insight and common sense. Hanani and Hananiah were earlier in charge of the palace and had proved themselves faithful in a smaller responsibility. Hence, they found favour with Nehemiah to be given the greater responsibility of leading and managing the city of Jerusalem.

Those who are faithful to the Lord are invested with a spirit of excellence as Daniel and his three friends were in the empire of Babylon. The Lord exalts those who love and honour Him above many others who are naturally more gifted or capable. He sees our faithfulness in lesser matters and gradually increases our influence and responsibility. He is a king who uses broken and weak vessels. He qualifies the unqualified. He has no use for the proud, arrogant and wicked. He honours and exalts the meek and faithful. He allows the stone that the wicked roll to roll back on them. He allows them to fall into the pit they dig for the godly and God-fearing.

The Lord desires that rulers not only be law-abiding but God-abiding. Once they have a personal relationship with the Lord, He gives them the grace or enablement to more than fulfil the needs and expectations of their position or responsibility. Faith gives God-fearing rulers confidence and hopes that they will succeed in whatever they do. Faith imparts a sense of vision and infuses deep values in leaders. It teaches them to learn from others, to learn from their failures and the mistakes of others. It keeps them from acting with a sense of selfish ambition or self-interest. They would not be egoistic. They would always act out of public interest and remain transparent and accountable to God and man for all their actions in the public domain.

62. THE LEADERSHIP TRIANGLE

"FOR GOD HATH NOT GIVEN US THE SPIRIT OF FEAR, BUT OF POWER, OF LOVE AND OF A SOUND MIND."

– 2 Timothy 1:7

The leadership triangle of power, of love and of a sound mind or self-discipline replaces the erstwhile spirit of fear in us. Our natural tendency is to fear. The power to overcome fear comes from God. He imparts the Spirit of might, of counsel and of the more wholesome fear of God. He gives us the strength to run and to finish the good race of life well. The leadership triangle consists of power or ability, of love or character and of self-discipline. The Lord pours His strength or grace in the areas of our weakness and imparts His glorious power in the areas of our strength. The Holy Spirit enabled the impulsive and emotional as well as undependable Peter the grace to overcome the areas of his weakness. He also enabled the spiritually blinded fanatical, one-track mind of Saul to see and experience the transforming power of the risen Saviour Jesus.

He enabled Peter who feared arrest and a cruel death by crucifixion like Jesus to overcome his fear of death and to lay down his life eventually as a martyr. He enabled Peter who did not want to reach out to the Gentiles or Non-Jews with the love of Christ to do so. He broke through mental and emotional barriers and taboos of social interaction. Fear holds us back from sharing the love of God with others. Fear holds us back from utilising all our talents and abilities for the glory of God. Fear of a lack of resources keeps us from trusting the Lord for our provision. Fear of our past haunts us in the form of guilt. Fear of the uncertainties of the future keeps us from taking risks or decisions. Fear keeps us from growing strong and mature in faith, but perfect love casts out all fear.

Our love for the Lord needs to be perfected or established by the Holy Spirit who knows what exactly holds us back. Faith does not mean a suspension of all our mental faculties but a fuller and more balanced use of our God-given wisdom and understanding. We need to discipline ourselves, our appetite, our attitudes and our habits. The Lord promises to help us or give us the grace or strength to do so. The fear of God keeps us from all evil while the love of God keeps us on the path of goodness and positivity. The One who inhabits us helps us deal with our inhibitions.

63. THE MANGER LEADER'S SOURCE OF POWER

"BEHOLD, A VIRGIN SHALL BE WITH CHILD AND SHALL BRING FORTH A SON AND THEY SHALL CALL HIS NAME EMMANUEL, WHICH BEING INTERPRETED IS, GOD WITH US."

– Matthew 1:23

God could have chosen to manifest His Son as a full-grown man but He chose Mary to be the surrogate to bear the holy child. He could have chosen to have His Son to be born into a family of great wealth, stature and influence but He chose a virtually impoverished family whose head was a mere carpenter. God wanted the Kingdom of God to begin as small as the mustard seed, to grow naturally to fill the whole earth with the knowledge of His truth and grace. The Kingdom of God is the government of God, by God, for God. God governance being better than good governance, His kingdom is ushered into the earth by Jesus being born as a normal human child though He is a mighty God, Prince of Peace, Wonderful, Counsellor and Everlasting Father.

His kingdom and therefore, manger leadership has the characteristics of power, peace, wonder, wisdom and of being for all eternity. A manger leader or manager does not just pay lip service to the idea of God but He is a living person indwelling in and with Him. Emmanuel or the God with us, in us, for us manifests Himself in a variety of ways in our day-to-day lives. Faith in the finished work of Jesus makes us worthy for God to dwell with us. Love of God in Christ produces good works in and through us. When God is in us, with us, for us, we can tap into His wisdom. We experience His power, might and unfading greatness. We will gain an understanding of the wonders of creation that we normally would take for granted. The rising of the sun will remind us of the birth of Jesus every single day. The Lord will counsel us through His Holy Spirit to do certain things and what we should avoid doing. We will daily experience His love, care, protection and provision as our Everlasting Father. Manger leadership and management proceed on the assumption that it is natural to be supernatural and spiritual since the non-physical parts of our being and life are created in the image of Christ. Jesus is the perfect image of God and the manger leader or manager endeavours to emulate Jesus, to model on Him, to be just like Him.

64. THE MANGER LEADER'S SOURCE OF STRENGTH

"FEAR THOU NOT, FOR I AM WITH THEE, BE NOT DISED, FOR I AM THY GOD. I WILL STRENGTHEN THEE, YEA, I WILL HELP THEE, YEA, I WILL UPHOLD THEE WITH THE RIGHT HAND OF MY RIGHTEOUSNESS."

– Isaiah 41:10

*T*he manger leader or manager has no fear. His confidence and trust are in God. He is assured of the Lord's presence with Him at all times, in the valley of the shadow of death as well as in the land of the living. The presence of God is the source of his strength, competence and resources. He humbles himself before God and entrusts all of his concerns, desires and challenges to the Lord. He knows that God is with him as an everlasting Father who will never leave him nor forsake him. He does not trust in earthly riches or power or position. He believes in the generous provision and absolute security the Lord provides. He knows he will never have cause for disappointment or regret as long as he walks in His light, His love, His integrity and His grace, as long as he reflects the "be happy" attitudes that Jesus extolled in the sermon on the mount, as long as he walks in truth.

The manger leader or manager recognises that God's grace is sufficient for. He knows that God who said He is the I AM can be all things he needs him to be. He believes in the justice and power of God as the Mighty One who will vindicate, deliver, extricate him, honour him and bless him abundantly. The manger leader does not however shirk his own responsibilities. He goes the extra mile to excel in whatever he does for he does it in the name of God. He lives by the credo of devotion to God, the dedication of all efforts to God, determination to set and achieve targets, discipline to control his own desires, emotions and actions and diligence in all matters.

The uni-verse promises that if there is a shortfall in anything, the Lord will help us. He will strengthen us in our resolve, our faith and our faculties. He will impart wisdom and guidance. If we fall short of our goals, He will support us. He will equip us to make good the gap. The manger leader or manager has an attitude of dependence on God and interdependence with other people. He uses all the God-sent opportunities. He employs all the available God-given resources. He does not suffer excessive stress or executive burnout as he never feels or acts as if he is overloaded. He is neither proud of his own strengths nor ashamed of his weaknesses as he has dedicated the former to the Strongest One, the Almighty and he considers his weaknesses opportunities for God to manifest His grace and power.

65. LEADERSHIP BY GRACE

"LET US THEREFORE COME BOLDLY UNTO THE THRONE OF GRACE THAT WE OBTAIN MERCY AND FIND GRACE TO HELP IN TIME OF NEED."

– **Hebrews 4:16**

*J*esus has by His death and resurrection absolved us by the first act of all sin and gives us hope of eternal life through His second act of rising from the dead. He is now at the right hand of the Father in heaven as our advocate, intercessor and High Priest. On account of this, we can enter boldly the court of the Lord and approach His throne to obtain both mercy and grace. Grace is beautifully defined or described in this uni-verse as the divine help God gives us in our time of need. The manger leader or manager's testimony is always, "I once was blind but now I see by grace."

A 'manger' leader or manager does not enter the presence of the Lord on his own merits but on the basis of the justification provided by Jesus. The word "justification" means to "make straight." The Lord is the One who has made our ways straight, our hearts straight. We live and walk in the "street called Straight." It is the narrow way. It is the more uncomfortable way. If we move a little to the left or the right, we will be hurt like Balaam the prophet on his "prophetic donkey." Jesus as our High Priest who once was fully human walked this narrow path and remained faithful and victorious till the end. Though vulnerable as humans, He proved Himself to be the Mighty God.

He did not yield to temptations or pressures. He knows our shortcomings and supplies what we lack with His abundant mercy and grace. Manger leadership and management is not about self-righteousness as there is nothing to be proud of in terms of our character or our abilities. It is leadership and management by grace. It involves boldness, courage, initiative, dynamism and confidence based not on our physical or intellectual attributes or expertise. It is not based on good luck or intuition but on the favour of the Lord. Like Jesus, the manger leader or manager grows in wisdom (Decisional Intelligence), in knowledge (Intellectual Intelligence) and in favour with God (Spiritual Intelligence) and man (Emotional and Social Intelligence). Decisional Intelligence is about making the right choices consistently and being able to identify at an early stage if one has made any wrong choice and take prompt steps to correct it or at least contain the damage. Since the Lord is the only One who knows the end from the beginning of everything that exists and will ever exist, He gives the manger leader guidance by way of prompters, pointers and markers through the ministry of the Holy Spirit and the shaping of circumstances.

66. FIVE DIMENSIONS OF BALANCED AND EFFECTIVE LEADERSHIP

"BUILT ON THE FOUNDATION OF THE APOSTLES AND PROPHETS, CHRIST JESUS HIMSELF BEING THE CORNERSTONE."

– Ephesians 2 V 20

The many so-called secular leaders or managers fail as they do not know how to manage their invisibles or their inner being. They do not have a model to emulate. They do not have the wisdom or knowledge to deal with the uncertainties of life, business and industry. They do not have a guide or coach or even laid down ground rules to follow in various circumstances. These shortcomings are met in the five titles and attributes of Jesus as specified in this uni-verse. Government or leadership and management challenges are met in Jesus. Life and leadership rest on His able shoulders for He is shaped as a cornerstone that holds the whole edifice in place. This uni-verse gives us the five dimensions of God governance manifested in Jesus.

Jesus is a Wonderful Governor. This is the supernatural dimension. He is both human and divine, natural and supernatural, miraculous and amazing. He best represents the perfect blending of the natural and the supernatural that the leader or manager should model on. He is a Counsellor, one who advises, guides, understands and comforts. This is the dimension of wisdom and understanding. Jesus is the Mighty God, this is the power dimension as well as the justice dimension. He holds the universe in place and ensures that the justice and righteousness of God are met in earth as in heaven. This dimension sees Him intervening on our behalf against powerful foes and enemies. He vindicates the righteous by faith. Jesus is also the Everlasting Father. This is the personal and love dimension.

This attribute sees Jesus caring for us as a loving Father, rebuking and correcting us when we go wrong or disobey the will of God, providing for us according to His riches in glory, protecting and covering us as a hen covers its chicks with His wings of prayer and the Word. As an everlasting Father, He has compassion on us. He intercedes with His Father in heaven on our behalf. The fifth dimension of leadership is peace. Jesus is the Prince of Peace. He purchases in His death the potential of peace with God for all. He destroys the works of darkness of the prince of darkness. He replaces the ruler of darkness in our hearts and gives us peace with our past, peace in the present, peace in the future and eternal peace.

He brings order and peace out of darkness, violence, chaos, sin, grief and sorrow. He commands the waves of every storm in our lives to be calm and these will obey His voice and Word. He restored and maintains peace

66. Five Dimensions of Balanced and Effective Leadership

in our inner being regardless of the circumstances. Jesus rules us as a Wise and Wonderful Leader, as a Sovereign and all-powerful God, as a loving, gracious, generous and redeeming Father, as a Prince who rules us not with fear or making us feel insecure and vulnerable but through peace and security. As leaders or managers, we too need to be aware of, possess and utilise these five dimensions of a sense of wonder, of seeking and using wise counsel, of using strength and power in the right way to accomplish what is just, of being like a gracious, merciful, generous, caring, protective father, of ruling to establish and enhance peace in our homes, offices, streets and nations.

67. THE IMAGE OF THE HUMAN LEADER

"SO GOD CREATED MAN IN HIS OWN IMAGE, IN THE IMAGE OF GOD CREATED HE HIM, MALE AND FEMALE CREATED HE THEM."

– **Genesis 1:27**

*D*o faith-based, scripture-based answers fill the gaps in the science-based questions that we ask like why did God create us? He created us to be like Him. We are therefore a created being who is to be like the Creator. We are not to cast Him in our image, rather He has cast or moulded us in His image. What are the characteristics of God? He is creative. We are to be creative. He is thoughtful. We are to be thoughtful. The scripture also says that God is love and so, we too are to be loving. God is Spirit and has no physical form. Hence, though we have a physical form, our essential nature is spiritual. We are to seek His kingdom, His character, His righteousness and His glory. God brings order out of chaos, form out of shapelessness, light out of darkness, water out of dryness, reason out of confusion and truth out of untruth.

We too are to be partners with Him and like Him in bring order, peace security and progress out of chaos and darkness. We are a blend of spirit, mind and body, of

67. The Image of the Human Leader

reason, emotion and action, of thought and imagination. When man first fell or sinned or came short of the standards of God, the image of God in us was distorted or corrupted. The divine faculties of reason, thought, emotions, imagination, action and reaction became distorted and used for purposes other than what God had designed us for. God out of His great love sent of His own, Jesus, the divine Being to be one like us in order to restore us to the fullness of the original image in which we were first created. We are to aim to be the living image of Jesus today for we were created in the image of Jesus. We should cast away every thought, word, emotion, action or reaction that distorts that image of Christ in us.

God created man and placed him in a garden. The word "garden" has hidden in it the phrase, "guard Eden." We need to guard our inner kingdom of thoughts, feelings and desires as our paradise or Eden. We need to guard our homes, our families, our cities, villages and nations as our Eden or outer paradise lest these become the den of thieves and robbers. We should use not only our reason but our imagination or the ability to project and create images of our own as God does. We are not only to be creative or innovative leaders, we are to be caring leaders or servant leaders like Jesus who subjected the exercise of power to the rule of love. We are to be cautious and prudent leaders in the Eden entrusted to us.

68. LION-LIKE LEADERSHIP

"THE REMNANT OF JACOB SHALL BE AMONG THE GENTILES IN THE MIDST OF MANY PEOPLE AS A LION AMONG THE BEASTS OF THE FOREST, AS A YOUNG LION AMONG THE FLOCKS OF SHEEP, WHO, IF HE GOES THROUGH, BOTH TREADETH DOWN AND TEARETH IN PIECES AND NONE CAN DELIVER."

– **Micah 5:8**

*T*hose who have a covenanted personal relationship based on commitment are the remnant of Jacob on whom the dew of the Lord's grace and compassion has fallen. Contrary to the general view that believers are weak or soft people, this uni-verse projects the image of great strength, power and leadership being manifested by the people of the house of Jacob. We are to be lion-like in our leadership qualities, fearless, bold, strong and dignified. A lion is fierce and aggressive even as a sheep is meek and yielding. We need to blend both these sets of qualities of sheep and lion even as Jesus is both a Lion of Judah and a Lamb of God. The enemy of our souls is described as a roaring lion. He is in other words an ageing lion who tries to intimidate people only with his roar but has lost his prowess or power. We who believe in contrast are young lions. A young lion never falls prey or victim to a roaring

68. Lion-Like Leadership

but aging lion. We should be ruthless with the roaring but aging lion and defeat or vanquish him in all of the strategies and traps he sets for us.

The lion-like qualities are not in terms of physical power or violence but in terms of spiritual strength and prowess. Jesus demonstrated such qualities of a lion when he cleansed the temple of merchants and moneylenders in righteous wrath. Hidden anger should simmer in us against the evil we see around us. It is not expressed in violence but in fervent spirit and all-conquering faith exercised in prayer and proclamation. The lion reflects the best regal qualities among all beasts of the forest. Likewise, we are to reflect the best qualities of Jesus in our everyday life. The metaphor of the young lion is used to emphasise that our faith and enthusiasm for the Lord and His Word should always be young and strong. We can tread upon all that is evil in this world with the power of the Holy Spirit in us.

We are to be watchful and alert like a young lion. A young lion is always at ease and in a state of poise or equilibrium as if nothing could disturb him. Our faith in the Lord frees us from stress and causes us to be self-assured, calm, relaxed and at poise even in difficult circumstances. A young lion is decisive and goes after its targets with a killer instinct. We, too should not vacillate or procrastinate but once a target is firmed upon, we should go after it with the speed and alacrity of a young lion.

69. THE SHIP CALLED LEADERSHIP

"HOLDING FAITH AND A GOOD CONSCIENCE, WHICH SOME HAVING PUT AWAY CONCERNING FAITH HAVE MADE SHIPWRECK."

– I Timothy 1:19

Paul draws the image of a faithful person as one who steers a ship called leadership. Faith is like holding the helm. A believer is a helmsman for the Lord as Noah was. He is to steer the ship over the ocean of life to the eternal destination, facing both good weather and stormy weather, calm seas and turbulence in the course of our lives, but always guided by the compass of the conscience. Writers like Stephen Covey refer to it as the moral compass and seeking the true North, but as believers, the needle of our conscience that has been enlightened by the light of salvation and the word of truth needs to not only point us to the north but also away from the south, our negatives, our weaknesses, our temptations, our limitations, our failures.

Temptations are like the mirages that a desert traveller sees. These are the rocky shores that can break up our ship. The Word is the lighthouse that warns us of the presence of these rocky shores and helps us chart our course. We are to prefer to face trials than to yield to temptations. If we do not follow the dictates of our good conscience or a conscience informed by the Word of what is good and what is bad, what direction is to be pursued and what is to be avoided, our faith would be shipwrecked. We are to anchor in the Lord and His Word from time to time while biding our time to press forward through the waves and ups and downs of life. Like a good ship captain, we should know our maps, as to where we are at a point in time and where we are heading.

A good conscience comes from pursuing righteousness following the example of the captain of our salvation, Jesus. A good conscience comes from acting on the basis of righteous principles expounded or implied in the Word of Christ. These principles provide the high mast and sails to pick up the wind of the Lord's favour. The message we deliver to the world is the ballast or cargo to retain in the ship's hold to provide balance during the voyage and to be delivered at different ports of call. The chief engineer on our ship is the Holy Spirit who reveals what part of our lives are functioning well or are malfunctioning. He keeps all the parts well-oiled and adds the unction to our function.

70. LEVEL GROUND LEADERSHIP

"TEACH ME TO DO THY WILL, FOR THOU ART MY GOD, THY SPIRIT IS GOOD, LEAD ME INTO THE LAND OF UPRIGHTNESS."

– Psalms 143:10

The ground we walk on determines the quality of our walk. The fool treads on sinking ground, the ignorant as well as the wicked on shaking ground, the wise on high ground and the faithful on holy ground. The godly walk on level ground. Level ground leadership is what the Lord provides to His flock. Level ground is the land of uprightness, integrity and righteousness. When we declare to God that He is our God, we enter into a personal relationship with the Father. We become God-fearing and Christ-loving. His good, holy, truthful and gentle Spirit will lead us onto the level ground so that we do not stumble or twist our ankles.

Level ground leadership implies that the Lord keeps us from stepping on the precipices of moral failure from which we will find it difficult to recover. He will teach us the art of decision-making such that our choices and decisions are in alignment not only with our long-term interests but the eternal will of the Father. Level-ground leadership

70. Level Ground Leadership

implies that the Lord will keep us from both pride and lust that corrupts the image and soul of leaders right through history. Level ground leadership happens when we are both able and stable. We do not act inconsistent with the beliefs and principles that we have been taught by the Lord and that we hold dearer than life itself.

The Lord directs the steps of the righteous. The Holy Spirit will whisper in our ears- take this step or go in that direction. Level ground leadership means that not only should we commit to learning what the will of the Lord is and do it but we need to be sensitive to hear His Word and His voice and obey it. Even if we stumble or make mistakes at times, the Lord will restore us to our feet. Not only do we learn from the Lord, but we also lean on Him for strength, power and grace to follow His steps, the path that He indicates to us. Like a leech sticks to a man's skin, we need to stick to the Lord and draw strength, wisdom and grace from Him. Like salt removes a leech from our skin, the Word must be used to remove sin and unrighteousness from our lives. Level ground leadership requires that our dependency on the Lord should be total and complete. Our obedience needs to be total and complete, not omitting even the details of what He asks us to do. If He asks us to speak to the rock, we should speak and not strike the rock. Our means are as important as the ends. The Lord justifies or sets right our means and our ends.

71. TRUE LEADERSHIP

"TRUST IN THE LORD WITH ALL YOUR HEART AND LEAN NOT ON YOUR OWN UNDERSTANDING, IN ALL WAYS SUMIT TO HIM, AND HE WILL MAKE YOUR PATHS STRAIGHT"

– **Proverbs 3 V 5, 6**

Only a true follower of God can be a true leader of men. Those who follow their own wisdom, their own ambitions or other people are blinded by ignorance, pride, arrogance, vanity, folly, greed and the like. A true follower of God listens to the commands of the Lord to love the Lord with all his heart and all his mind and all his strength. He diligently studies, understands and remembers the principles embedded in the Word of God. He is not guided by divisive human ideologies of the left or the right. He has a clear vision, a sense of focus and priorities. He uses all the gifts, talents and resources he has been given to accomplish his task. He occupies strategic heights so that he can maximise his influence and impact on people and organisations. He is not deterred by difficult or tough circumstances but keeps moving on with faith and confidence in the Lord.

Headship or leadership is promised to the true follower of Christ. He is meant to lead, influence and serve. He will be listened to. He is lifted above the level of

71. True Leadership

politics of nations. He is not motivated by ideas of self-glory or grandeur. He puts into practice the precepts of life taught by Jesus. He emulates the example of Jesus in all things. He knows he can do nothing on his own and all things by the grace of Christ. He recognises that His power flows from anointing and not from appointment. He is bold, brave and confident by the power of the Holy Spirit. His communication and conversation are pleasing to the Lord.

The true follower of Christ is a constant learner. He is growing in his knowledge of Christ and His love. The wise men followed the star over the manger in Bethlehem while the wise followers of Jesus follow Him, the star of history and the star of the Kingdom of God on earth and in heaven. He does not merely observe and understand what is written in the Word but He is a doer. He implicitly and explicitly obeys the Lord. He corrects his own personal flaws as he sees them in the mirror of the Word. If he lacks wisdom or strength, He asks with faith and obtains it from His leader and King. He is not interested in the loaves and fishes of office. He focuses his attention on pleasing the Lord and winning the eternal prize, the wreath of victory that will not fade with time.

72. THE PATTERN OF AUTHORITY AND POWER

"JESUS CAME AND SPAKE UNTO THEM, SAYING, 'ALL POWER IS GIVEN UNTO ME IN HEAVEN AND ON EARTH.'"

– Matthew 28:18

Jesus was in a position of some power while He was ministering to people and healed many of all kinds of diseases affecting the mind, the eyes, the ears, the skin, the nerves, the blood and the heart. He also demonstrated power over nature when He commanded nature over the stormy Sea of Galilee. Even when He was arrested He demonstrated His power by restoring the severed ear of the servant of the High Priest that had been cut off in anger by one of his disciples. In the days that followed and on the cross as He was dying, He submitted Himself willingly to a position of no power like a lamb that is about to be slaughtered, but, after His resurrection, He confirmed that all power of heaven and earth was given to Him.

Jesus, the Christ or the anointed One to first do the good news of salvation and then announce it, had become Jesus Christ, the Lord and King of Kings. Jesus is sovereign over all the earth, the heavens and Heaven itself. He had come into His own as the Lion of Judah. He has power and

72. The Pattern of Authority and Power

authority over the living and the dead. He is raised to the right hand of the throne of the Father and He is exalted far above every principality, power, might, dominion, authority and far above every person or creature named in this world and in the world to come. His power and authority vest in His very name and when we invoke His name, that power and authority are released. All power and authority of Jesus vests in the Holy Spirit who is now God on earth administering, guiding and leading on His behalf.

Jesus today has power over life and death, over all diseases, over all mishaps, over all contests and competition, overall struggles and conflicts, over all creatures and all people, over all angels and demons, over all spirits, over the past, present and future. All things in heaven and earth were delivered to Him to administer and rule. It lies in His province to decide whom to save and whom not to show mercy to. It is His discretion to delegate His authority and power to whom He chooses. He spoke this universe to His disciples to begin the process of transforming them from mere disciples or learners to apostles. No longer did they have to fear what humans can do to them. No longer were they to fear their persecutors however high and mighty for the One who sat over them had commissioned them and given them His authority and power.

Jesus as the firstborn of God, the Father has the authority to execute judgment on earth and in heaven on behalf of the Father. He has power over all flesh and has the authority to give eternal life to whomever He chooses. Jesus fulfils the prophetic Word that came from Daniel of a stone that is not cut with human hands that destroy the power, authority and grandeur of successive kingdoms and empires of the earth and fills the earth with Zion, the mountain of the Lord. The significance of this uni-verse for believers is that we who are powerless have derived authority and power from Jesus's impartation. He has imparted the anointing of His authority and power upon us to execute judgment on the earth, to preach the good news of deliverance and eternal life to the brokenhearted, to proclaim liberty to spiritual captives, breaking every bondage and setting them free by the truth that is Jesus.

73. PATTERNS OF LEADERSHIP

"LET THE WORD OF CHRIST DWELL IN YOU RICHLY, TEACHING AND ADMONISHING ONE ANOTHER IN ALL WISDOM."

– **Colossians 3 : 16**

*T*he keywords and phrases in this uni-verse are, God's Word, and His teachings. The key actionable words or verbs are "to believe" and "to obey". In a co-related verse in concordance to this verse, it is written that "the ancient and honourable will be the head and the prophet that tells lies will be the tail." The Lord promises leadership or headship to those who believe Him, study and delight in His Word and obey Him in the world. The connection between belief in God, diligence in study, preparation and actions leads to leadership. Belief in God distinguishes the wise from the fool, the leader from the follower and the sighted or the visionary from the short-sighted or blind.

Stephen Covey wrote about Principle-centred leadership and it was widely acclaimed, but, in the light of this uni-verse, if a person is not principle-centred or Word-Centred, he or she cannot be classified as a head or leader. Even a prophet or a man of God who lies is considered only a tail or a follower at the fag end of the totem pole of leadership. Principles that we need to follow in life flow from the Word of God. There is no other earthly or heavenly source. Power, authority, influence, wisdom and security flow from these godly principles extracted like gold from its ore. For the past several years, day after day, I have attempted to extract these godly principles of life and leadership and share them with the world and my readers.

If we pay attention to what God says, we will have no tension. He will guide us precisely on the paths we have to take. He will not lead us down a path of red herrings as the enemy of our souls does right from the beginning of time. Once we hear or read what God says, we need to study, analyse and understand it. Once we understand it, we need to apply it or commit it to our hearts to obey or do it. Mere 'head knowledge' or theoretical and unapplied knowledge does not make one a leader. Leadership requires a transfer from head to heart, a distance of about twelve inches. These twelve inches make all the difference to our lives and to the lives of those who follow us.

The uni-verse promises headship or leadership to the ones who faithfully follow this process all their lives. I was anguished to hear that some of the top leaders in the modern world whom I greatly admired have been exposed due to some failings and flaws in their leadership patterns. This again underlines the need for godly leaders and leaders of this world to be trained equally in using or leveraging on their strengths and overcoming weaknesses, threats and temptations. There are some qualities of the tail in all of us. Only the kangaroo's tail is strong enough to support it when it stands and propel it in motion. We

73. Patterns of Leadership

need to turn our weaknesses using the grace of the Lord to strengthen our tails or in other words, turn the leadership potential destroying the power of weaknesses into a source of strength. It is possible when we carefully observe and do the cautions and precautions and counsel of the Lord contained in His Word. The scripture is written on this binary pattern, "Cling to what is good, let go of what is evil." It implies that we should cling to what is held up as good in the Word and let go of what is evil as held up in the Word.

74. THE LEADERSHIP MANTLE

"BLESSED IS THE ONE WHO PERSEVERES UNDER TRIAL BECAUSE, HAVING STOOD THE TEST, THAT PERSON WILL RECEIVE THE CROWN OF LIFE THAT THE LORD HAS PROMISED TO THOSE WHO LOVE HIM."

– James 1 : 12

*H*eadship or leadership is due to what the Lord accomplishes in and through us. It comes as a blessing for our devotion to Him. Devotion to God is synonymous with diligence in reading, remembering, meditating, applying or obeying His Word. Obedience is not just something that happened in our past but a daily heeding to the Word. The promise follows such daily application of the principles of the Word in our lives, we shall excel in all that we do. We will exceed expectations. To observe His commands is to serve Him. He then pours His grace on us so that we can lead others through service. Jesus Himself came to be the head of all humanity by His diligence in knowing, understanding and obeying the Word even the hard parts related to His allowing Himself to be put to a cruel death for the sake of all.

Hence, headship or leadership does not mean a life of privilege or success as the world understands it. Our lives will not be in vain but they will fulfil the purpose for

74. The Leadership Mantle

which we are created and sustained by the Lord. We may not be Very Important Persons but we will certainly be Very Significant Persons. Diligence with the Word does not mean only studying it but in doing or carrying it out in practical ways in our lives. It is not a theoretical or theological or head knowledge that we are called by this uni-verse to possess but a 'heart knowledge', a love for the Word since it comes from the Lord. The Word transforms us from within like nothing else can.

The top that the Word refers to is not in terms of position or power but that we will be a "Tabernacle of Peace" (ToP), a servant of the Prince of Peace, Jesus. We will experience Shalom or multi-dimensional, comprehensive and holistic peace all the days of our lives. We will have ups and downs, highs and lows in our days and our lives and we will go through thick and thin but through the various circumstances, such complete, incomprehensible peace will be our concomitant or constant companion.

75. THE ALPHA OF DOMINION

"GOD SAID, 'LET US MAKE MAN IN OUR IMAGE, AFTER OUR LIKENESS AND LET THEM HAVE DOMINION OVER THE FISH OF THE SEA, OVER THE FOWL OF THE AIR, OVER THE CATTLE, OVER ALL THE EARTH AND OVER EVERY CREEPING THING THAT CREEPETH UPON THE EARTH.'"

– **Genesis 1:26**

Dominion means leadership. God made man in His image or His likeness with the mental, moral and social capacity for leadership of all other species. Like God, we can think, plan, create, communicate, judge, desire righteousness and know right from wrong. He placed everything else under the feet of man but man alone He placed directly under His own leadership. Since Jesus is the visible image of the invisible God, human beings are created in the image of Jesus. Therefore, our highest aspiration is to be or become as close as possible to the character of Jesus. Just as all other species are placed under the dominion of man, all mankind is placed under the dominion or leadership of Jesus. Just as all other species are tamed by man, our powerful organs and parts of life that are made in the likeness of God, our intellect, our

75. The Alpha of Dominion

tongues, our spirits, our attitudes, our talents and gifts are tamed, trained and used by Him.

No one else in all of history fills this space as adequately as Jesus then and now. He is the prototype or model. We too are expected to be types of Christ even as Abel, Moses, Joseph, the apostles were types of Christ who either preceded Jesus on earth or followed after Him. Love is the essence of godly or Christ-like dominion or leadership. When we resist the dominion or leadership of God in our lives, we are kicking the thorns or in other words, hurting ourselves needlessly and pointlessly. When we yield to the leadership of God in our lives, we are uplifted, edified, ennobled, enabled, equipped and empowered. The Spirit of God dominates or rules over our thoughts, emotions, actions and reactions. We have the inner strength to endure great trials, difficulties, challenges and tests in this life.

Knowing what is right from wrong in the eyes of God and consistently seeking what is right is the trait of good and godly leaders. Dominion is to be first sought over one's own self before we can lead or rule others. Dominion or power or influence is not sought for its own sake as the world's leaders do but in order to pursue what is right and to avoid what is perceivably wrong. Great power and influence are released from the hands of the Lord onto, into and through the godly leader. He can command the elements of nature even as God can. His Words have immense creative power. He has dominion over his own emotions, desires and motives. He voluntarily surrenders the dominion of his life either to the enemy of our souls or to the Lord God.

Jesus demonstrated through His own leadership style that dominion is not for abuse, exploitation or domination but to serve, to heal, to teach, to uplift, to encourage, to exhort, to warn, to build, to develop, to set free, to equip and to enable. All of our power, our gifts, our faculties, our talents, our opportunities and our resources are to be used likewise to serve God and our people. Our power over nature is to be also used with a sense of responsibility and restraint.

76. THE ALPHA OF KINGSHIP

"YE ARE A CHOSEN GENERATION, A ROYAL PRIESTHOOD, A HOLY NATION, A PECULIAR PEOPLE, THAT YE SHOULD SHEW FORTH THE PRAISES OF HIM WHO HATH CALLED YOU OUT OF DARKNESS INTO HIS MARVELLOUS LIGHT."

– I Peter 2:9

Unlike the Philosopher-King concept of Plato, the Priest-King is not in a constant quest for answers to his questions but has found most of the answers settled in Christ. In Christ, we not only claim and have a kinship with God but we inherit kingship. We are kings and priests in the sight of God. We are priests to declare His praises for choosing us out of our generation, separating us from the darkness and drawing us into the marvellous light of truth, power and love that emanate from His presence and His Word. As kings, we have to reign on earth, reining in the powers of darkness. As kings, we proclaim His greatness and aspire to magnify His name on earth. As kings, we execute justice, peace and righteousness in all we do. As kings, we expand His dominion and influence of the Kingdom of God. As kings, we act always with a sense of dignity as behoove royalty.

As priests, we conduct ourselves such that we are blameless and holy in all we say, think or do. The power of the king in us is derived from the foundation of the holiness of the priest. Together, as royal priests, we have unassailable and unshakeable authority on earth. As kings, we exercise power while as priests we seek wisdom. As priests, we offer sacrifices of praise and thanksgiving since Christ has obviated in His death on the cross the need for any more sacrifice of life. We offer the sacrifice of Abel. We offer ourselves as living sacrifices, setting aside our own desire for glory or greatness, our own priorities and our lusts. We no longer revel in the works of darkness that we formerly used to enjoy. As priests, we intercede for those who now live in spiritual darkness.

We claim and declare healing for the sick and afflicted. We become instruments to bring comfort to the hurting and deliverance to those in need of it. As Ministers of God, we have different portfolios or responsibilities to execute here on earth. We study His laws and see how best to carry these out in our lives. The paradox is that as kings under the King of Kings, we are placed above all the kings and authorities of this world but as priests, we are servants of all mankind. As kings of God, appointed and anointed by Him, He supplies all we need to govern or to rule. As kings of God, we are required to bring more of heaven on earth and more of the earth into heaven. We take steps to end disorder and lawlessness here on earth and usher in the peace and rule of God.

We are extraordinary people with extraordinary gifting, qualities and powers. We are a holy nation placed above all the nations of the world to seek, speak and execute the will and Word of God. The standards, motives

76. The Alpha of Kingship

and values that we espouse are distinct from the children of this world. As priests, we make confessions to the Lord for our own shortcomings and those of others. As priests, we wear the robe of salvation while as kings, we don the armour of God. As Sons and Daughters of God, we have supernatural abilities or gifts of the Spirit, supernatural characteristics or the fruit of the Spirit.

77. THE ALPHA OF THE TRUE LEADER

"NEITHER BE YE CALLED MASTERS, FOR ONE IS YOUR MASTER, EVEN CHRIST."

– Matthew 23:10

This uni-verse clearly states that just as we have one Father, the One in heaven, so also we have one Master or Leader on earth, Jesus. We should not be presumptuous to call ourselves leaders or teachers for we have only one Leader and Teacher revealed from heaven, the Lord Jesus. We should rather regard ourselves as servants of the Lord. This runs counter to the trend worldwide as believers and workers in the Vineyard of the Lord take pride in calling themselves and getting others to recognise them as leaders by taking on various designations and titles like apostles, bishops, prophets, leaders and so on.

Jesus taught His disciples that it is better to be the servant of as many as possible rather than lording it over others even as He gave Himself as a ransom or payment for everyone. The more people we are serving, the more we lead to the Leader the greater our calling and our anointing or enablement. Jesus declared Himself to the Way, the Truth and the Life. Jesus proved it through His Words and His deeds. He proved Himself to be the true Master

77. The Alpha of the True Leader

as He washed His disciple's feet, the true Leader for He led by example and the true Teacher for He knows the eternal truth. He overcame the temptations of this world. He overcame death. He overcame the consequences or penalty of sin. Hence, sin could not hold Him, prisoner, in the grave. He is the only One who imparts His resurrection power to us. He left the Holy Spirit to lead, build, guide, comfort, counsel, encourage and strengthen us.

78. STELLAR LEADERS IN POLE POSITIONS

"DO YOUR BEST TO PRESENT YOURSELF TO GOD AS ONE APPROVED, A WORKER WHO DOES NOT NEED TO BE ASHAMED AND WHO CORRECTLY HANDLES THE WORD OF TRUTH."

– 2 Timothy 2 : 15

*T*he Lord created man for "dominos" or headship and leadership but we need to first accept Him as our immediate and ultimate Leader. God revealed or manifested Himself as the leader of humanity in the coming in flesh and blood of His Son, Jesus. Jesus is the password to life, leadership, management, the Passover from death to life, from darkness to light, from folly to wisdom, from ignorance to knowledge, from curses to blessings, the passport to heaven, the Kingdom of God or the rule of God on earth. As the password, He unlocks the secrets of life and leadership. As the Passover, He has paid the price, the cost of purchasing eternal life for us. As the passport, He gives us instantaneous access to the presence of the Lord. Jesus is the way for leaders to excel.

When we give priority to the Word of God daily, when we carefully study and observe or obey the commands and believe and claim the promises of the Lord, we are equipped

78. Stellar Leaders in Pole Positions

to be leaders. The Bible is certainly the best leadership training material and the best leaders in world history like Abraham Lincoln, Mahatma Gandhi and Mother Teresa have been deeply influenced by it. They learnt how to avoid the pitfalls of leaders by avoiding the failures and mistakes of biblical leaders and likewise, to emulate a good example of Jesus and other leaders. They did not swerve to the right or the left but stayed on a course like arrows till they hit the target or the objectives set for them or set by them. Power, even absolute power would not corrupt such leaders for their hearts are always tuned to be right with God, to be meek even if powerful.

The uni-verse tells us that we are destined for leadership and not just ordinary leadership but for the top positions or the pole positions. It also tells us the Lord plays an active and continuous role to move us into the top positions. Before He does that He prepares, trains, enables and equips us to be faithful leaders as He did with Moses, Joseph, Gideon, Deborah and many other biblical leaders including the apostles of Jesus. We are not meant to be tail-enders or the insignificant leaders who hold up the tail but the frontline leaders. We are not losers but winners and overcomers. We do not run away from responsibilities or challenges. We tread difficult paths in order to encounter the impossible in the end. Circumstances might change at the toss of a coin but our commitment will not flag. Heads, we win. Tails, also we win, but what we desire most is to win souls for the Lord.

79. ABSOLUTE POWER THAT DOES NOT CORRUPT

"YOU WILL TREAD ON THE LION AND THE ADDER; THE YOUNG LION AND THE SERPENT YOU WILL TRAMPLE UNDERFOOT."

– Psalm 91 v 13

*J*esus had sent seventy followers in pairs out into the cities and villages to bear the good news of salvation. They were overjoyed to see that even demon-possessed people were delivered at their word of command uttered in the name of Jesus. "Serpents and scorpions" are harmful spirits or demons that exploit the vulnerabilities and weaknesses of man. When the 70 followers reported back, Jesus saw the vision of satan falling like a lightning from heaven, meaning that the authority of satan over mankind was broken. He no longer ruled over the world. The word "authority" comes from the author. The author of a book has absolute right and power over the characters and content of his book. Likewise, Jesus, the Author of life has the authority to bless, to heal, to deliver, to command, to rebuke. He not only has the authority or power but He has delegated it to His followers to exercise it in His name.

Jesus revealed the authority of God by commanding spirits and healing all types of diseases and even altering or changing substances like He did by changing water to wine in the marriage at Cana and multiplying bread and fish to feed the multitude. He gave His followers the faith and the authority to exercise such power over the demonic spirits. The authority is like a blank cheque pre-signed by Him for the uni-verse states, "Over all the power of the enemy." He removed the sense of fear and apprehension of His followers that the spirits could harm or retaliate by saying, "Nothing will in any way harm you." He sought to empower and equip His followers to do greater things than even He did on earth. We too should empower those we lead to do greater things than we could ever do instead of projecting ourselves as unique and non-pareil.

The sign of a true leader is such confidence that they are not threatened by the growth of their followers. Rather Jesus was overjoyed that their faith and spiritual knowledge had matured enough for them to challenge the deceptive authority and power of satan. Jesus gave His followers the authority to bless those who welcomed them and to withdraw that blessing when they did not. The latter He forewarned would have unpredictable consequences. Hence, one should not mess with someone who can bless us. Jesus told His followers that the ones who listen to them are listening to Him and the ones who are listening to Him are listening to the Father. In this manner, He connects us with the omnipotent power and enabling grace of God, El Shaddai. We can pronounce blessing in His name and also rebuke in His name. The spirits would flee when we rebuke in the name of Jesus. We are to exercise such authority and the Lord will preserve us from all harm. Even lifeless objects as well as the dead will obey the authority Jesus gives us. Hence, He said, "If you have faith as small as a mustard seed, you can command a mountain to move." Faith like a seed does not remain small but keeps growing and we realise we have the authority or power to face bigger and bigger challenges even in the spiritual realm.

80. FEEDING THE FLOCK

"FEED THE FLOCK OF GOD WHICH IS AMONG YOU, TAKING THE OVERSIGHT THEREOF NOT BY CONSTRAINT, BUT WILLINGLY, NOT FOR FILTHY LUCRE, BUT OF A READY MIND."

– I Peter 5:2

A leader's task is not to lead but to feed the flock. We become the flock of the Good Shepherd when we listen to His voice and invite Him into our hearts. Thereafter, we grow to resemble sheep and the Good Shepherd Jesus in two aspects, humility and gentleness. We grow to maturity by living by every Word that proceeds from the mouth of God. We grow to become shepherds ourselves who feed the young lambs as well as the mature sheep the Word of God. The Word is our daily manna. "Manna" has a hidden meaning, "Man, now apply." The time to obey the Word is now not later, to put into practice whatever the Lord speaks or teaches us from His Word.

We should not lead the sheep reluctantly or with the wrong motives of profiting from it financially. Freely we have received and been taught. Hence, freely we should give and teach. We should not use the influence we have over the "flock" to manipulate them, to discourage them but to encourage, edify and build their faith in the Good Shepherd. We must study, analyse and absorb the Word so that it saturates our minds. Our minds become the very mind of Christ and we learn to think, interact and speak graciously and wisely as Jesus. We are able to then give an apt answer to anyone who questions our faith or desires to clear his or her own doubts.

Initially and for some time, the flock can be fed "milk" or what is easily digestible by them but as they grow, they need more solid food that will strengthen their "spiritual bones", so that they exercise their own "faith muscles" more rigorously. They are trained in righteousness or the application of spiritual principles and precepts contained in the Word so that they become skilled workmen and the Word is a tool in their hands to help them handle any situation of life in an able and stable manner. We as well as those we are teaching or discipling become equipped for every good work. The Holy Spirit stands alongside us and guides us as we do the work of shepherds. He does not teach us all of it in one shot but line by line, precept by precept.

81. TO LEAD WITH DILIGENCE, TO SERVE WITH JOY

"HE WHO ENCOURAGES, IN THE ACT OF ENCOURAGEMENT. HE WHO GIVES, WITH GENEROSITY. HE WHO LEADS, WITH DILIGENCE. HE WHO SHOWS MERCY, WITH CHEERFULNESS."

– **Romans 12:8**

We have a different calling in accordance with the natural and spiritual gifts the Lord has endowed in us. We are to exercise the gift in proportion to our growing faith and His unlimited grace. The picture St Paul draws is one of the interdependence of the body of Christ, the spiritual church just as the different members of the body depend on each other. We are not given these gifts to be used only for our benefit but for mutual benefit. Some are called to be in the ministry of encouragement. Barnabas the disciple who replaced Judas was known as an encourager. Some are called to bless others with giving and they need to give generously as the Spirit leads.

Some are called to be leaders, godly leaders. They need to lead with diligence. They need to study the patterns of the leadership of the Lord, the leadership of the patriarchs, the leadership of the kings of the Old Testament and the leadership of the apostles and emulate their models. They should not spare any efforts to groom, shape and mould those who follow them by example and precept. Leadership on the pattern of Jesus is servant leadership, not meant to dominate and be served but to serve the led. Such leaders should also study the models that we should avoid, the pitfalls of leadership that we should pre-empt, the weaknesses that should be overcome and the challenges of human nature that should be confronted.

We should care for others ungrudgingly as if we are caring for ourselves. Our attitude, while we are doing all these things, is as important as what we do. We should show such care, not with a wearisome but with a cheerful attitude. Apparently, it is impossible to do all this without the grace of the Lord. He anoints, equips, empowers and enables us. We should return again and again to the Lord to draw from Him both stability and ability. Some of the tasks and goals we confront are far beyond our human abilities but the Lord will lend us wisdom, power, resources, people and the ability to execute them by His grace.

82. CONTRASTING MODELS OF LEADERSHIP

"I AM AFRAID THAT, EVEN AS THE SERPENT BEGUILED EVE BY HIS CUNNING, YOUR MINDS BE CORRUPTED AND LED AWAY FROM THE SIMPLICITY OF YOUR SINCERE AND PURE DEVOTION TO CHRIST."

– 2 Corinthians 11:3

*B*oth the serpent leader and the servant leader are spiritual leaders but present contrasting models of leadership with different motives, methods and results. The serpent leader is extremely cunning. His chief goal is to cause people to stumble and fall. The servant leader is sincere and devoted to fulfilling the purpose set before Him by the Father. The serpent leader can be very persuasive and has a range of tricks up his sleeve to deceive, convince and persuade people. The servant leader is convicted with simple truths. The serpent leader mixes good with evil and serves it up as something attractive to humans. The servant leader is absolutely sincere, pure and truthful. His Words are spoken not from the cunningness of the mind but the bottom of His heart.

The serpent leader's goal is to divert people from being devoted to God, to attempt to rob the glory of God and to throw doubt on the authenticity of the servant leader. His modus operandi is duplicity. He causes people not only to doubt the Word of God but to be double-minded and to live a double life, to be one thing in public and quite another in private. The serpent leader reads people like we read books. He knows our shortcomings and how to exploit them. The servant leader helps us overcome our weaknesses and shortcomings and enables us to neutralise our threats. The serpent leader corrupts people while the servant leader refines and purifies people to present them blemishless before the Lord.

One day, I heard of the double life being led by someone many of us respected over the years. He was reputed for his knowledge of the Word, but unknown to even his family, the serpent leader beguiled him into believing in his immunity, that no one would know if he had a secret extramarital relationship with a series of women. The discerning now say that pride had first taken root in his heart before he succumbed to sexual temptation. The serpent leader sends his pet little foxes of pride, envy, bitterness, hatred and folly into the vineyard of the faithful's heart and tries to destroy the fruit of the Spirit. The servant leader guards us against such predatory emotions and motives. The servant leader builds our hearts as a tabernacle of joy, a temple of peace for the Lord to inhabit, to reside and preside over our lives. The serpent leader rejoices when we fail when we are defeated while the servant leader rejoices when we succeed when we are victorious in our struggles of life. The servant leader helps us at all times with His wonderful counsel and His strength.

83. BE A MENTOR, NOT A TORMENTOR

"THE THINGS WHICH YOU HAVE HEARD ME TEACH IN THE PRESENCE OF MANY WITNESSES, ENTRUST TO RELIABLE AND FAITHFUL MEN WHO WILL ALSO BE CAPABLE AND QUALIFIED TO TEACH OTHERS."

– 2 Timothy 2:2

St Paul in this verse was charging or commissioning Timothy whom he had mentored. Likewise, we who are followers of Christ need to entrust the work of sharing God's truths to others. The precepts, warnings and doctrines are priceless treasures that equip people for every life situation, including facing death in a pandemic. The qualities of the mentees are enumerated by Paul as reliability, faithfulness and the ability to teach others. He places credibility before ability and qualities before qualifications. Timothy was first exhorted by Paul to be strong and empowered by the grace of Christ Jesus. He called him to lead a life of discipline and endurance of hardship that might come his way. The grace of Christ is sufficient to empower and equip us with the abilities we need to be witnesses for Him in this world, but, we also need to work hard on our skills as communicators and leaders of the flock.

We should keep enriching our understanding with insight into the precepts and truths of life and of God. Matters of faith are not taught just orally but by example. Paul emphasises that the truths were imparted in the presence of many witnesses to show that he lived by the principles and precepts he taught. He practised what he preached so that people saw the truth in action, impacting, healing, delivering and changing lives all around. This is the way, Jesus, the Teacher of teachers taught, by consistent faith, practice, discipline and with the authority and grace of God.

84. THE ROLE OF GODLY LEADERS AND PROPHETS

"THEN ZERUBBABEL THE SON OF SHEALTIEL AND JESHUA THE SON OF JOZADAK AROSE AND BEGAN TO REBUILD THE HOUSE OF GOD IN JERUSALEM AND THE PROPHETS OF GOD WERE WITH THEM, SUPPORTING AND ENCOURAGING THEM."

– Ezra 5:2

Zerubbabel, before whom the mountains were made plain, was a descendant of King David. The mountains, implying huge challenges, were not flattened by natural or physical strength but by spiritual authority, power and prayer. Kings, today are a metaphor for leaders in different spheres of life. We might face several huge challenges in building the Kingdom of God but we will be able to overcome them by the grace of God. Leaders should never forfeit the grace of God by thoughtless lifestyle, arrogance, by relying on their own wisdom and intellect, strength or connections. Our worldly adversaries will raise obstacles in our paths but the Lord will help us remove them, one by one. Leaders do not plough a lonely furrow. The Lord will send prophets to encourage and support leaders even as He sent Haggai and Zechariah to encourage Zerubbabel.

Unlike Zerubbabel, we are not attempting to build a physical temple, but even as Jesus referred to His own body as God's temple, we are to build the temple inside of us. The Word and our actions in alignment with the Word are the bricks and mortar we use to build this spiritual temple. There may be many irritants, obstacles, problems, barriers and setbacks but the Lord will enable us to face and remove these by one. Whatever we build to honour God, we must have Jesus as its cornerstone who is connected to all we are, say and do. The entire edifice of our lives rests on Him. He is the foundation on which we build our lives as a testament to God. When we have this perspective, nothing we do or say is in vain. God plus us is infinite. God minus us is also infinite, implying that with God all things are possible for us, nothing is impossible. Without Him, nothing is possible for us.

85. BRAND NEW LEADERSHIP

"THE LORD SAID TO SATAN, 'THE LORD REBUKE YOU, SATAN! INDEED, THE LORD WHO HAS CHOSEN JERUSALEM REBUKE YOU! IS THIS NOT A BRAND PLUCKED FROM THE FIRE?'"

– Zechariah 3:2

A godly leader is a brand plucked from the fire of the Lord. He is purified by the Word, by teaching, by the fire of experience and by the fire of the Holy Spirit from the dross and impurities of lust and pride of this world. He has the authority of the Lord upon him. Using this authority, he can rebuke satan. He can pray and restore Jerusalem from its ruined conditions, overrun by invasions. Jerusalem literally means, The Peace of the Jews. Jesus is the Prince of Peace. Hence, when the Jews recognise that Jesus is the Prince of God, the Son of God, the promised Messiah whom they were instrumental in crucifying on the Roman instrument of execution, the cross, then the peace of the Jews, Jerusalem will be restored. Satan does not have the power or authority to accuse a person who has been purified by the fire of God. He is a brand plucked from the fire.

He is a brand-new creation. Hence, no accusation of the enemy of our souls can prosper against us, no tongue can stand against us. We have the authority and anointing of Christ to judge and rebuke satan and his agents. We have been by the grace of Christ plucked from the fire of hell, from the fire of destruction, from the fire of God's anger. Now, we rest under the shelter of the Lord. He is our strong defence. Since we are a brand plucked from the fire, we can face the world with courage and boldness, we can face adversity, endure and overcome it and we can face our earthly foes and spiritual enemies and emerge unscathed and victorious. Today, the word "brand" is touted as a symbol of quality, of excellence, of moving towards zero error. Hence, we as God's brand and as His ambassadors should stand for quality, truth, for excellence in all we think, say and do. We are a brand chosen by the Lord by His grace. We enjoy the brand new life in Christ and we are brand new leaders. The Jews as a race and as a nation are chosen but we who believe and trust in the name of Christ are chosen as individuals, not for our personal qualities or achievements. The Lord has gone through the ordeal of fire for our sake and He has chosen us to bear His name, to suffer for His name, to bring glory to His name.

86. THE AUTHORITY OF THE AUTHOR OF LIFE

"HE BEGAN SAYING TO HIM, 'BY WHAT AUTHORITY ARE YOU DOING THESE THINGS, WHO GAVE YOU THIS AUTHORITY TO DO THESE THINGS?'"

– Mark 11:28

The episode of the chief priests and scribes questioning Jesus's authority to preach, teach, cleanse the temple, forgive sins, heal diseases, multiply food and drink and bring the dead to life is reported in all four gospels. Jesus had in the preceding days cleansed the temple of money changers and traders, saying with righteous anger, "My House shall be called a house of prayer and you have turned it into a den of thieves." He had acted apparently with authority. They questioned Jesus's authority to find a way to put Him to death for blasphemy. Jesus answered them with a counter question, "By what authority did John the Baptist baptise people in the Jordan?" The priests and scribes debated among themselves and chose not to answer the question sensing they would fall into the trap that they themselves had set for Jesus.

Jesus discerned the motive behind everything spoken to Him. Likewise, we should be discerning enough to get behind the thoughts or motives that undergird the words of people. The events that preceded and followed confirmed that Jesus got His authority from the Father in heaven. The word "authority" comes from "author". The Father along with the Son (the Word that is from the beginning) and the Holy Spirit had brought all things in creation into being. Only the Creator or Author has the power to bring about change in the destiny and character of the creation. Authority implies both responsibility and power.

Jesus as the Author of creation and of human beings has both power and responsibility for the well-being of all humans even as earthly authorities have both the power to rule over citizens and a responsibility to serve them, protect them and fend for them. Jesus proved through His many acts and words that He had authority over nature, He commanded the waves and winds and they obeyed Him to be still. He has authority over life. He commanded the dead to come alive. He has the authority to forgive, He forgave the sinners. He has the authority to heal, He healed people of all types of diseases. He has the authority to rebuke, to chastise, to punish, He rebuked the Pharisees and teachers of the law who laid heavy burdens on the common people that they were not authorised to do. He has authority over death for He was Himself resurrected.

He has the authority to call people to serve God. He has the authority to teach, to instruct, to lead, to deliver. We, ourselves who follow Jesus have no authority of our own other than what He has given us. We pray in His name, we exercise authority in His name. We command, rebuke, serve, bless, forgive and teach only in His name.

86. The Authority of the Author of Life

Therefore, Paul wrote that we should fix our eyes on Jesus, the Author and Finisher of our faith, the One who began and perfects our faith. We need to focus on Jesus, the locus or centre of history, of the universe, of heaven. Only an author has the right to change the story or the script he is writing. Likewise, only Jesus has the right to alter our destiny and our character to bring glory to God.

87. ABILITY WITH STABILITY

"THE SERVANT SAID TO HIM, 'LOOK HERE, IN THIS CITY IS A MAN OF GOD AND THE MAN IS HELD IN HIGH HONOUR, EVERYTHING THAT HE SAYS COMES TRUE. NOW LET US GO THERE PERHAPS HE CAN ADVISE US ABOUT THE JOURNEY AND TELL US WHERE WE SHOULD GO.'"

– I Samuel 9:6

*S*aul, the son of Kish, a man of considerable wealth and influence who belonged to the tribe of Benjamin was in search of something mundane like his father's donkeys. Sometimes, when we too lose something, the Lord may be leading us to some higher ground. When they were frustrated about not finding the donkeys that had strayed away, the servant of Saul advised him to meet the prophet and man of God, Samuel.

Likewise, when we are reaching a dead end in any of our pursuits, we should seek out the man of God who can pray and counsel us. Samuel had already received an intimation the day before of a young man of the tribe of Benjamin who would be anointed king of Israel. The people of Israel wanted a king like all other neighbouring lands.

87. Ability with Stability

They did not heed the warnings of the Lord given through Samuel that any human king would exploit them, mislead them and abuse power and privilege, but as the people insisted and wanted to go beyond the perfect will of God, the Lord allowed His permissive will to operate. The Spirit of the Lord rested on Saul who was head and shoulders above his peers in his personality and ability. The lesson we learn from the example of the kings of Israel recorded in the scriptures is that for good leadership, we need to have mental ability coupled with emotional stability. We will have the ability and stability only if we rely on the leading of the Spirit of the Lord and depend on His Word to lead and guide us in all our ways.

Power will then neither tempt us nor corrupt us. Some of us are to play the role of Samuel to be kingmakers or those who anoint leaders for our nations in different realms. The Lord will anoint us as seers or prophets to the nations and what we say will come true. As a result, people will honour and respect us, knowing that the Lord is with us and favours us with His wisdom and grace. They will come to us for something as mundane as the loss of something valuable in their lives, to find out how and where they should continue their journey of life.

88. INTUITIVE LEADERSHIP AND WISDOM

"IN THE DAY OF PROSPERITY BE JOYFUL, BUT IN THE DAY OF ADVERSITY CONSIDER. GOD ALSO HATH SET THE ONE OVER AGAINST THE OTHER, TO THE END THAT MAN SHOULD FIND NOTHING AFTER HIM."

– Ecclesiastes 7:14

When times are good, enjoy. When times are bad, endure. Our lives are like the alternating squares of black and white on a checkerboard. When we are on the white or symbolically good times, we got to prepare for the black. When we are in the black, we need to live in hope of the white. Joseph's dream of seven years of prosperity and plenty followed by seven years of famine and scarcity set the course of policy in ancient Egypt so that they stored enough grain during the years of plenty. The role of intuition in effective leadership is a less researched subject. Genius is one per cent intuition and 99 per cent tuition. We need to factor in the gut instinct, the urging and prompting of the Holy Spirit and even the dreams and signs we see and experience for we are spiritual beings and quite unlike the animals who only exist to eat, drink and sleep. We should be able to interpret the signs and signals we receive.

88. Intuitive Leadership and Wisdom

We cannot know the future in its entirety but we can find pointers and divine guidance. Once we read the signs and signals correctly, we can learn from the experience and knowledge of others about how to use the special or rare insight that we have discovered intuitively. During times of prosperity and peace, we should be thankful and rejoice in the Lord, but we should know that it will soon end and that we should build up the strength and reserves we need to endure during times of hardship and scarcity. Since even our fortunes are so fickle, we should consider and realize that only the Lord is consistent, faithful and dependable. We should ask ourselves during the good times, "What is it the Lord wants me to do?" and during the bad times, "What is it that the Lord wants me to learn."

The deep etch of our character is more etched by the chisel of the pain of adversity than by oodles of pleasure of plenty. The only other effective teacher of character other than the pain of adversity is the eternal Word along with prayer and prophetic ministry. As we live by every Word that has proceeded from the Word of God, we will receive intuitive wisdom. The way God has set up everything in our lives ends up in a zero-sum game where in the end we gain and lose nothing, the only prize we can win for eternity is the crown of eternal life.

89. WONDERFUL POWER, AUTHORITY AND GOVERNMENT

"FOR TO US A CHILD SHALL BE BORN, TO US A SON SHALL BE GIVEN AND THE GOVERNMENT SHALL BE UPON HIS SHOULDER, HIS NAME SHALL BE CALLED WONDERFUL COUNSELLOR, MIGHTY GOD, EVERLASTING FATHER, PRINCE OF PEACE."

– Isaiah 9:6

This uni-verse is spoken as if Mary and Joseph were saying it many centuries after Isaiah wrote the prophecy. Everything about Jesus is Wonderful, the prophecy nearly a millennium before, the conception by the Holy Spirit of a yet unmarried young woman and the immaculate or virgin birth without human intervention. The prophecy was not that He will be part of the government of the Kingdom of God on earth but that the power and the responsibility of government squarely rested on His shoulder. He was named ahead of time. His titles were given ahead of time, Wonderful Counsellor, Prince of Peace, Mighty God and Everlasting Father.

No human would ever have such titles. The last title given to Jesus is Lord Amen in the Book of Revelation,

89. Wonderful Power, Authority and Government

implying that He had fulfilled the prayer and hope of all people. He is the One who causes all prayers to be heard and answered. To focus on just one word WONDERFUL, "Jesus possessed and he still possesses wonderful wisdom beyond His age and the ages." His attributes and qualities are wonderful. His Words were wonderful. His actions were wonderful. His miracles are wonderful. The greatest miracle He did when His body was dead was when His Spirit did the impossible of impossible by raising Him from the dead. Each miracle had a meaning and a purpose. He changed water into man, proving his mastery over matter. He is the Master of the Banquet of life and can provide what we need. He healed the royal official's dying son. He has power over disease. He filled the fishermen's empty nets with fish. It proved He can provide abundantly. He cast out an unclean spirit, proving His authority over demonic spirits.

He healed Peter's mother-in-law of fever instantly by just holding her hand. It proved His touch could heal even less deadly sicknesses. He healed a leper, proving He can cure the incurable. He healed the centurion's servant, proving He could just speak the Word and people would be healed. He raised the widow's son, proving He has authority over death. Jesus did many other wonderful miracles, He stilled the storm, proving He has authority over the fury of nature. He cured the man possessed by many evil spirits, proving He has authority over all spirits and they obey Him. He cured the paralytic after forgiving His sins, proving His authority to forgive sins. He resurrected the synagogue leader's daughter by taking the girl's hand proving His touch could resurrect the dead. En route, when a woman with bleeding touched the hem of His robe, she was instantly healed, proving that His touch could heal anyone even secretly. He healed two blind men who called out to Him, proving He could restore sight wonderfully to the blind. He healed a mute man, proving He has the authority to restore speech and hearing.

He healed a man who was invalid for 38 years, proving He has authority over chronic diseases. He healed a man with a shrivelled hand, proving He has the authority to heal, restore and make whole any withered part of anybody. Jesus fed five thousand people with five loaves and two fish, proving that He has the authority to multiply scarce resources. He healed a Canaanite woman's daughter of demon possession, proving He had compassion for any human regardless of religious or racial background. He healed a deaf man, proving that He has authority over hearing and can heal by just speaking one word, "Ephphatha" or open. He healed a blind man by just applying a salve of mud and spit, proving that even His saliva has healing power. He healed a boy with epileptic fits due to demonic possession, proving He could set free anyone from physical as well as spiritual ailments. He healed a man born blind, proving that He can heal even the physically challenged who have a handicap from birth.

He healed a man of dropsy or physical swelling of his body, proving He can heal any inflammation. He healed ten lepers, proving He can heal people individually or in groups and He can heal the incurable. Jesus raised Lazarus from the dead after three days, proving it is

89. Wonderful Power, Authority and Government

never too late for Him to act or heal or resurrect the dead. Jesus's Words to the fig tree caused it to wither to its roots, proving the fierce power of His judgment, too. Jesus healed the high priest's servant's severed ear, proving He can restore even dismembered organs miraculously. He forgave the prostitute showing that His mercy and compassion are as wonderful as His power and authority to counsel, heal, restore, judge and resurrect. No one in any human government anywhere has such power, authority, compassion and wisdom. Hence, He is called WONDERFUL.

90. THE AUTHORITY OF JESUS

"THEY SAID TO HIM, 'TELL US BY WHAT KIND OF AUTHORITY YOU ARE DOING THESE THINGS? OR WHO IS THE ONE WHO GAVE YOU THIS AUTHORITY?'"

– Luke 20:2

*T*hen as today, people question the authority of Jesus. Is the source of His power or authority to do the unthinkable, the unimaginable and the impossible from man or God? Jesus refused to answer this question of the chief priests, elders and scribes for the answer was obvious. It lay in the very scriptures that they were studying. Jesus represents God for He is the visible expression of the invisible God. He is the Author of life as we know it. We are created by Him, through Him and for Him. Hence, He was exchanged as a ransom for our sake. History got bifurcated by His act of sacrifice for mankind into the dark ages before and the age of the coming of His light into this world.

Jesus in the course of His brief life on earth of 33 years proved He has authority over demons, diseases of all kinds including the deadly, the incurable and the inherited ones, over the elements of weather, over human beings, over angels, over the mind, over matter, over death and

90. The Authority of Jesus

sin, over time, over principalities and powers of darkness. By His mere word on many occasions, He commanded all of these at various times. No human before or since has demonstrated an iota of His total power and authority. Yet, He exercised it not flamboyantly but with responsibility, wisdom, grace, humility and discernment and only when needed and natural means were not enough. He did not, however, monopolise His authority and power but shared it with His followers. Just as God authorised Him to do the miraculous and supernatural, He authorised His first disciples as well as contemporary ones to do greater things than these. His authority being vested in His name makes it possible for us to speak, command, heal and deliver people. He has given us the authority or keys to both heaven and earth and we exercise it through prayer and intercession. The testimonies of people around the world right through history who were healed, delivered and blessed in a variety of ways are proof of the continuing authority of Jesus. He continues to shape and influence our lives for good.

91. BEING SPIRIT LED

"FOR IF YOU ARE LIVING ACCORDING TO THE IMPULSES OF THE FLESH, YOU ARE GOING TO DIE. BUT IF YOU ARE LIVING BY THE POWER OF THE HOLY SPIRIT YOU ARE HABITUALLY PUTTING TO DEATH THE SINFUL DEEDS OF THE BODY, YOU WILL REALLY LIVE FOREVER."

– Romans 8:13

*I*f we are led by the Spirit of God, we are children of God. If we are children of God we will be led by the Holy Spirit. The Holy Spirit will empower and enable us to habitually put to death sinful impulses of the body. We will not live according to the dictates of the latter- the impulses but we will subject or submit ourselves to spiritual leadership. Our souls are freed from the natural law of entropy or the bondage to decay inherent in all matter. Our bodies are subject to decay and death but not our spirits when we are led by the Holy Spirit. When we are led by the Holy Spirit, He will fill our hearts and minds with love instead of lust, with humility instead of pride. Instead of the spirit of fear, we will have the spirit of adoption or the spirit of the children of God. Instead of slavery to sin and consequent guilt and curse, we begin to enjoy the glorious freedom of the children of the house and not the enforced fear of

91. Being Spirit Led

servants or slaves of God's household. We enjoy the rights and blessings of being co-heirs with Christ.

If we are called to enjoy the privileges and rights of inheritance with Christ of the Father's kingdom, we are also called to share in the fellowship of suffering that Christ underwent for our sake. The suffering purifies and perfects our faith. We begin to perceive the value of being led by the Holy Spirit and not follow our own whims or impulses. The Holy Spirit teaches and guides us on how to pray and how to lead our lives. He shapes our inner being so that we are transformed and conform to the image of the firstborn- the Son of God, Jesus.

92. AUTHORITY OVER THE SERPENT LEADER

"LISTEN CAREFULLY, I HAVE GIVEN YOU AUTHORITY TO TREAD UPON SERPENTS AND SCORPIONS, OVER ALL THE POWER OF THE ENEMY AND NOTHING WILL HARM YOU."

– Luke 10:19

*T*he seventy followers of Jesus were sent out to minister into various cities and towns before He himself went there. He sent them in pairs with the authority to heal, to deliver from demons in His name. They came back and reported joyfully that the spirits obeyed them when they spoke in His name. The self-same authority is vested in every believer of Jesus. We have authority given us by the Author of life and of salvation over all the power of the serpent leader. The Servant Leader Jesus has given us authority over all powers of darkness or the powers of the serpent leader. Every time we kneel to pray or claim in faith a promise or obey a command of the Lord, we are crushing the head of the enemy.

Every time we pray, rebuke or command the spirits, satan falls like lightning from heaven. The book of Acts records the miracle when Paul is bitten by a serpent or snake. People expected him to swell and die with the

92. Authority over the Serpent Leader

poison but Paul just shook off the snake and nothing happened to him. Likewise, as long as we are living by faith, the serpent leader cannot harm us. We are granted that kind of spiritual immunity from every attack of the enemy. However, Jesus warns us not to be overjoyed at our power and authority over the powers of darkness but to be joyful that we are saved by His grace and mercy.

Other Books in this Series Available on Amazon:

1. The Key to Divine Blessing
2. The Quest towards The Unseen
3. The Creator's Wisdom Unveiled

My Personal Website

www.prateepphilip.com, www.friendsofpolice.net, www.fillipisms.com

www.ingramcontent.com/pod-product-compliance
Lightning Source LLC
LaVergne TN
LVHW091635070526
838199LV00044B/1080